UNDERGRADUATE RESEARCH IN FILM

A Guide for Students

Lucia Ricciardelli
MONTANA STATE UNIVERSITY

Jenny Olin Shanahan
BRIDGEWATER STATE UNIVERSITY

Gregory Young
MONTANA STATE UNIVERSITY

Routledge
Taylor & Francis Group
NEW YORK AND LONDON

First published 2020
by Routledge
52 Vanderbilt Avenue, New York, NY 10017

and by Routledge
2 Park Square, Milton Park, Abingdon, Oxon, OX14 4RN

Routledge is an imprint of the Taylor & Francis Group, an informa business

Library of Congress Cataloging-in-Publication Data
Names: Ricciardelli, Lucia, author. | Shanahan, Jenny Olin, author. | Young, Gregory (Professor of music), author.
Title: Undergraduate research in film : a guide for students / Lucia Ricciardelli, Jenny Olin Shanahan, Gregory Young.
Description: New York ; London : Routledge, 2019. | Series: Routledge undergraduate research series | Includes index.
Identifiers: LCCN 2019015047 (print) | LCCN 2019018329 (ebook) | ISBN 9780429485596 (ebook) | ISBN 9781138599512 (hardback) | ISBN 9781138599529 (pbk.)
Subjects: LCSH: Film criticism–Study and teaching. | Motion pictures–Study and teaching.
Classification: LCC PN1995 (ebook) | LCC PN1995 .R48 2019 (print) | DDC 791.4301071–dc23
LC record available at https://lccn.loc.gov/2019015047

ISBN: 978-1-138-59951-2 (hbk)
ISBN: 978-1-138-59952-9 (pbk)
ISBN: 978-0-429-48559-6 (ebk)

Typeset in Bembo
by Integra Software Services Pvt. Ltd.

UNDERGRADUATE RESEARCH IN FILM

Undergraduate Research in Film: A Guide for Students supplies tools for building research skills, with examples of undergraduate research activities and case studies on projects in the various areas in the study of film, film theory, film production, history of film, and interdisciplinary projects. Professors and students can use it as a text and/or a reference book. Essentially, what makes this volume unique is that it brings together examples of film projects and film studies courses within the framework of research skills.

Following an overview chapter, the next seven chapters cover research skills including writing literature reviews, choosing topics and formulating questions, working with human subjects, collecting and analyzing data, citing sources, and disseminating results. A wide variety of sub-disciplines follow in Chapters 9–16 with sample project ideas from each, as well as undergraduate research conference abstracts. The final chapter is an annotated guide to online resources. All chapters begin with inspiring quotations and end with relevant discussion questions.

Lucia Ricciardelli is Associate Professor of Film Studies at Montana State University.

Jenny Olin Shanahan is Director of Undergraduate Research at Bridgewater State University, with leadership positions in the Council for Undergraduate Research.

Gregory Young is Professor of Music at Montana State University and has held ongoing posts in conferences in undergraduate research and in curriculum development.

Routledge Undergraduate Research Series
Series Editors: Gregory Young, Montana State University, and Jenny Olin Shanahan, Bridgewater State University

Undergraduate Research in Music
A Guide for Students
Gregory Young and Jenny Olin Shanahan

Undergraduate Research in Art
A Guide for Students
Vaughan Judge, Jenny Olin Shanahan, and Gregory Young

Undergraduate Research in Dance
A Guide for Students
Lynnette Young Overby, Jenny Olin Shanahan, and Gregory Young

Undergraduate Research in Film
A Guide for Students
Lucia Ricciardelli, Jenny Olin Shanahan, and Gregory Young

www.routledge.com/Routledge-Undergraduate-Research-Series/book-series/RURS

CONTENTS

SERIES FOREWORD

The Routledge Undergraduate Research Series was created to guide students and faculty, particularly in the arts and humanities, working on a wide variety of research and creative projects. After a brief overview, chapters on the research process common to all disciplines follow, and then several chapters that pertain specifically to the discipline. The National Conferences on Undergraduate Research have expanded annually since 1987 to about 4,000 participants. The British Conference on Undergraduate Research has been an annual event since 2011, and the World Congress on Undergraduate Research started in 2016, demonstrating the relevancy of this movement in our changing higher education curriculum.

We are grateful to Ann-Maria Sylvia, Bridgewater State University graduate student (and former undergraduate researcher), for creating the index for this book and several others in the series.

Gregory Young and Jenny Olin Shanahan
Series Editors

PREFACE

The Expansion of Undergraduate Research

Initially led by science professors needing help in laboratories, undergraduate research (UR) activity in American colleges and universities has been increasing dramatically over the last 40 years. Thanks to national organizations such as the Council on Undergraduate Research (CUR) and the National Conference on Undergraduate Research (NCUR), these activities have been spreading rapidly into all academic disciplines. Even though CUR was started in 1978 by university chemistry professors as a way of collaborating with undergraduates in their research labs, at the present time, the biggest division of CUR is in the arts and humanities. NCUR, which began in 1987 as a celebration of UR in any discipline, currently registers about 3,500 student-presenters and 500 faculty mentors annually. In 2011, the first British Conference on Undergraduate Research (BCUR) was held, and it continues annually with the recent addition of Posters in Parliament, modeled after Posters on the Hill in Washington, DC. The Australian Conference on Undergraduate Research (ACUR) started in 2012, and Australia also has currently Posters in Parliament. The first World Congress for Undergraduate Research (WorldCUR) was held in Qatar in November 2016.

The primary reason that UR has spread throughout the world in every academic discipline is that it directly benefits students in a host of areas. Students who participate in UR are more likely to persist in college and graduate on schedule. They demonstrate significant gains in valuable skills such as critical thinking and analysis, oral and written communication, and logic and problem-solving. Additionally, student researchers report increased self-confidence, excitement about their field of study, and clarity about future goals. The benefits of participating in UR have been so well established that the Association of American Colleges and Universities has identified it as a high-impact practice—one of the key aspects of a college education shown to make a significant positive difference in the lives of students (Brownell & Swaner, 2010; Kuh, 2008). Although UR benefits students from every demographic group, major, and type of institution of higher education, first-generation and underrepresented minority students show the greatest gains (Brownell & Swaner, 2010; Linn et al., 2015). Overall, researchers concur that the advantages of participating in UR are most directly linked to the opportunities it offers for students to work closely with their professors in meaningful and profoundly interesting ways.

Despite decades' worth of evidence that UR is one of the most transformative pursuits a college education can provide, the majority of UR opportunities continue to be highly selective (often only for honors students) and limited to students in the laboratory sciences. In other words, research has not been the main focus, at least with undergraduates, in the art disciplines, where creative activity abounds.

About This Book

We wrote this book to help faculty and students in the arts, and film in particular, become more accustomed to viewing what they do through the lens of "undergraduate research," especially when a more inclusive sense of scholarship and creative activity is included. The acronym URSCA, which refers to Undergraduate Research, Scholarship, and Creative Activities, is seen by many as a more fitting way to talk about and recruit students to such opportunities. Creating opportunities for film students to participate in URSCA offers them access to a high-impact practice that may improve their cognitive and emotional development, acquisition of highly valued skills, and preparation for postbaccalaureate opportunities.

This book is organized in two large sections. Chapters 1–8 cover some of the fundamentals of research methods, many of which are common to most disciplines and the different subject areas in film. They provide a foundation to help students get started in understanding research protocols and processes. Chapters 9–16 cover UR in film subjects that are taught in many collegiate film schools. Chapter 17 provides annotated online resources, but certainly not an exhaustive list. Each chapter begins with inspirational quotes, a chapter summary, and then an explanation of the substance of the chapter with examples and ideas for film students to pursue. Many of the chapters have examples of abstracts submitted to conferences by undergraduate researchers in film across the United States.

Film majors, from their first semester until they take their capstone course, can use this book as a tool to build awareness about conducting scholarly work in the broad fields of film production and film studies. In a senior "capstone," not only can it serve as the course textbook, it can also be used as a more specific guide for the whole process of choosing a film topic and seeing it through to completion. Completing successful UR projects in film and disseminating the results at conferences, in publications, and film festivals will promote this activity and serve as a model for other film students in the future.

Students: How to Use This Book

A brief glance at the table of contents reveals that this book does not necessarily have to be read in order, from the first chapter to the last. Instead, it is intended as a guide to be consulted throughout the different facets of student research projects in film. There is no one perfect way to progress through a UR experience in film, especially because there are so many different areas to explore. Research in film studies, for example, is quite different from research study in the various technical aspects of film production. Therefore, with the guidance of your instructor, use the tools in the first half of the book (Chapters 1—8) as needed for your research/creativity, and read about a wide variety of student examples in the film areas that interest you in the second half of the book (Chapters 9–17). Be sure to glance through the online resources and delve more deeply into those online sites and audiovisual files that interest you. It might also be helpful to create your own set of online resources and have that handy for future reference.

Faculty: A Sample Upper-Division Film Seminar

FILM 301: Issues in Lens-Based Media at Montana State University School of Film & Photography is a junior-level seminar for students enrolled in our new Bachelor of Fine Arts (BFA) program in Integrated Lens-Based Media (AY 2018–2019). The course provides a methodological and critical foundation for the BFA degree, introducing students to seminal writings in the history, theory, and philosophy of film, photography, and related media. The goal of this course is to provide a space and time for students to reflect seriously and deliberately upon various manifestations of lens-based media—that is, of visual art produced by means of devices that focus the direction of movement of light and capture the resulting information. Students are prompted to consider both connections and differences in the forms, traditions, and styles of various lens-based media, with particular attention paid to issues of time, stillness, and motion. This will, in turn, enable students to produce more sophisticated lens-based media art products. As a seminar, the weekly, three-hour meeting will emphasize discussion and debate. Many of the assigned readings are challenging, and often highly theoretical, requiring ample time for exploration and interpretation. Over the course of the semester, students will complete a progressive sequence of assignments that build towards the completion of an audiovisual research essay.

Learning Outcomes

This course is designed to equip students with the critical tools necessary to understand, analyse, and critique the multifaceted and ever-shifting relationship between different forms of lens-based media. Students will:

- Acquire a critical appreciation of some of the principal concepts, methods, and debates informing the theory and practice of photography and cinema.
- Understand and articulate connections between and differences in the forms, traditions, and styles of various lens-based media, with particular attention to issues of stillness, motion, and time.
- Understand the convergent influence of digital technology on previously distinct analogue imaging media.
- Be able to research and evaluate relevant theoretical and historical materials for the study of lens-based media.
- Be able to interrelate texts and discourses specific to lens-based media with issues in the wider context of cultural and intellectual history.
- Demonstrate, through the creation of audiovisual essays, appropriate research and bibliographic skills, and a capacity to construct a coherent, substantiated argument through audiovisual means.
- Demonstrate, through research, discussion, oral presentations, and essay writing, a capacity to questions assumptions, to distinguish between fact and opinion, and to reflect critically on their own learning process.

References

Brownell, J. E. & Swaner, L. E. (2010). *Five high-impact practices: Research on learning outcomes, completion, and quality*. Washington, DC: Association of American Colleges and Universities.

Kuh, G. (2008). *High-impact educational practices: What they are, who has access to them, and why they matter*. Washington, DC: Association of American Colleges and Universities.

Linn, M. C., Palmer, E., Baranger, A., Gerard, E., & Stone, E. (2015). Undergraduate research experiences: Impact and opportunities. *Science*, *347*(6222): 627–633.

1

OVERVIEW

I have a way of filming things and staging them and designing sets. There were times when I thought I should change my approach, but in fact, this is what I like to do. It's sort of like my handwriting as a movie director. And somewhere along the way, I think I've made the decision: I'm going to write in my own handwriting.

Wes Anderson

Images are intrinsic to digital storytelling's communicative possibilities. Students use images to construct arguments connecting theory, history and story in their projects.

Digital Storytelling Multimedia Archive

Summary

This chapter outlines the undergraduate research environment and where the study of film fits into it, reframing some of the excellent creative work already being done in college and university film schools as faculty-mentored scholarship. Within this context, ideas are shared as to the importance of undergraduate research, desired learning outcomes, and how knowledge and audiovisual storytelling are created in the field of film. As readers of this book will realize, conducting research is certainly not limited to the sciences and related fields. Selecting and exploring a film topic, whether for the production of a movie or for the writing of a paper, can in fact be linked to the scholarly process otherwise known as *undergraduate research*. Undergraduate research is an interactive pedagogy that has been shown to be more engaging and successful than traditional classroom lecture-style learning.

Where Film Fits into the Undergraduate Research Movement

As learning in college becomes more active, and students desire greater input into their own education, undergraduate research, scholarship, and creative activities (URSCA) have become more significant. Since search engines like Google can help students find a plethora of content, and video-sharing sites such as YouTube and Vimeo provide a great array of video clips, films, and instruction at our fingertips, learning how to actually create knowledge, how to tap into our creativity, and how to advance the discipline of film, should take center stage, so to speak.

An undergraduate film degree, therefore, would not be complete without a substantial exploration into the discovery of knowledge in any variety of topics, from the way films are produced to theoretical and historical revelations or rediscoveries in the field of film studies. Film majors should be engaged in innovative techniques, analyses, and practices throughout their degree programs. Although in-depth study is often undertaken in the latter part of an undergraduate program, ideally students should be exposed to the act of discovery and creation as often as possible through the whole film program. Early and frequent opportunities to think with creativity, imagination, and originality have been shown to influence further successful learning and study.

When students are asked about their vision for how they would like to learn, many say they want it to be exciting, applicable, social, and interactive. Doing group projects, working alongside professors, having input instead of passively listening, and helping to chart their own pathways, can all be components of undergraduate research in film. When employers are asked what kind of skills they want future employees to have, many list teamwork, creativity, problem-solving, critical thinking, as well as written and oral communication. All of these can be strengthened by a real academic experience in undergraduate research and creative activity.

There are many different terms for "research," including inquiry, scholarship, creative activity, and creative scholarship. These terms are sometimes used interchangeably, though scholars in various disciplines often have preferences for the ways they describe their work. Many people involved in the Council on Undergraduate Research (CUR), especially in its Arts and Humanities division, use the acronym URSCA: undergraduate research, scholarship, and creative activity. Whether you prefer one term over another, or your university has a program that uses certain terms, the term itself does not matter as much as what it indicates: scholarly work that is faculty-mentored, original, disciplinarily appropriate, and disseminated (Osborn & Karukstis, 2009). We generally avoid some of the specifically scientific terms such as *hypothesis* and *methodology* when producing a film, for example, using substitute terms such as *background research, preproduction, production* and *postproduction stages*, and *stylistic techniques*. Students of film or any other field also benefit from the cross-pollination that occurs when considering how undergraduate research is practiced in disciplines that are quite different from their own, and when they explore the different terminology.

Opportunities for Original Research in Film

How can students do something original when professors, scholars, filmmakers, theorists, and other media practitioners have already done so much research in the fields of film production and film studies? One way is to take an interdisciplinary approach, viewing film from the perspective of another discipline. For example, there has been little research published on the correlations between film and biology, film and engineering, and film and computer science. Also, the collaboration between film and education studies offers topics that are ripe for discovery, especially with new widespread interest and increase in the use of digital audiovisual storytelling by education faculty members and students. One example of this kind of interdisciplinarity began in 2014 when an education professor named Christine Rogers Stanton (Education Department, Montana State University (MSU)) approached me (Ricciardelli) and asked me for advice about filmmaking equipment she wanted to purchase for the Blackfeet Community College (BCC) in Browning, Montana. This led us to an ongoing interdisciplinary collaboration, *The Digital Storywork Partnership* that has engaged BCC, Buffalo Hide Academy (BHA), Plenty Coups High School (PCHS), and MSU students and faculty in the creation of audiovisual counter-narratives (2015–today). Our goal has been to promote intercultural partnership and mentorship while developing BCC, BHA and PCHS documentary filmmakers (Stanton, Hall & Ricciardelli, 2017; Stanton, Ricciardelli & Hall, 2017). Thinking about other possibilities for interdisciplinary collaborations, what subjects could be paired with film? Chapter 10 of this book is focused on interdisciplinarity.

Students do not have to follow such an interdisciplinary path, however. There are many standard activities in undergraduate film programs that students and professors have been engaged in for decades that have not been generally regarded as undergraduate research. An example would be analyzing a short film that was shot with analog technology and then using it as a model to create a digital interactive film. Almost every campus now has some sort of annual undergraduate student research symposium, and while they were formerly focused on scientific research, they are increasingly campus-wide events open to students of all majors. This change has been accompanied by a parallel movement towards greater involvement by students in independent research mentored by professors, as well as projects that assist in or complement faculty research. The symposia that feature student research presentations sometimes consist solely of posters, where film students have to try to fit their presentation into a science-based format. On some university campuses, a variety of delivery modes are available, including film screenings, oral presentations, and multimedia installations. Whatever the format, with a little creativity, film students should be able to present in a way that allows them to communicate the results of their work effectively. Many universities and colleges are now stressing the importance of undergraduate research campus wide, and students in most disciplines are doing research as a regular part of their education and presenting their findings publicly. Film majors, likewise, benefit from joining in. Campus-wide celebrations of undergraduate research are still dominated by the sciences and related fields. These symposia could be enhanced with greater contributions from the arts, including a variety of film projects. And directors of such events are often open to the idea of adding special venues for film-related projects and allowing different methods of delivery.

Can Undergraduate Research Benefit Both the Student *and* the Professor?

More and more, universities are emphasizing the integration of scholarship and teaching, linking student learning with the discovery of knowledge, and making active learning a hallmark experience of an undergraduate degree. One of the best ways to accomplish all of this is to have a professor carve out a small piece of his/her own larger research project, and assign it to a student. Examples abound in chemistry, where researchers can be much more productive in the laboratory with the help of undergraduate researchers, and the students learn the complex process of original research in their field. In the arts and humanities, and particularly in film, professors often view their research/creativity as individual scholarly pursuits, and published articles and film and multimedia productions are usually listed with only one author/filmmaker. However, with a little creativity, win-win situations can be created that increase productivity for the professors and that provide firsthand experience on the front lines of the creation of art or original research for the students. An example occurred when I (Ricciardelli) enrolled an undergraduate researcher in spring and summer 2018, Michael Peterson, to help design, implement, and co-lead two documentary filmmaking workshops at the Stone Child College (SCC) at the Chippewa-Cree Reservation in Box Elder, Montana. The workshops were meant to impart the basics of producing a documentary film to SCC students in order to give voice to the oral stories of the Chippewa-Cree community (Egan, 1989; Stanton, Ricciardelli & Hall, 2017). The resulting product was a documentary short about the spiritual

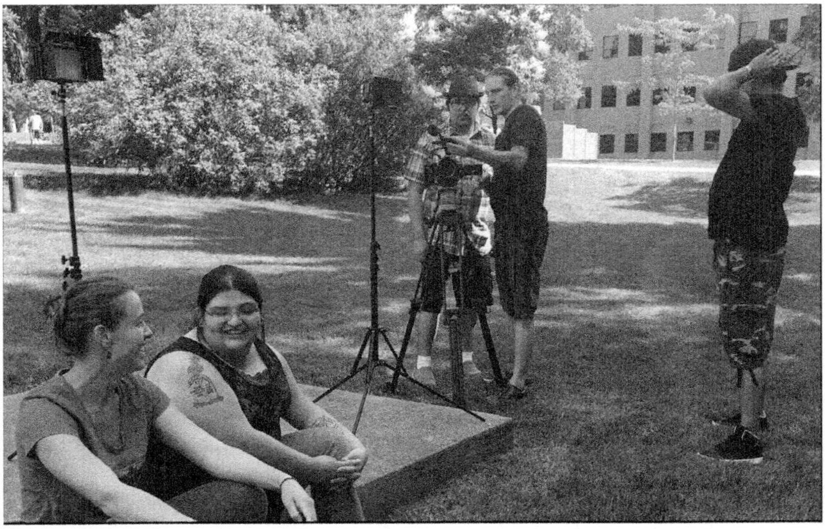

FIGURE 1.1 Michael Peterson and BCC students during one of the workshops at MSU-Bozeman (July 2018).

purpose of reservation dogs (*Rez Dogs*, which is currently in postproduction). This would not have been possible without this teacher–student collaboration, and Michael was able to list these teaching and creative activities on his résumé (see Figure 1.1).

Upper-Division Film Seminars

University film curricula usually offer upper division film seminars in the junior and senior years, with titles such as *Studies in Film* (covering a wide variety of topics in the theory, history, and criticism of film), *Documentary Production, Fiction Film Production, Theater Production*, and *Senior Production*. Although not often referred to as undergraduate research, these most often are exactly that. For example, students writing a film script are required to perform background research, be knowledgeable about human behavior, and craft their own treatment; students studying direction and cinematography need to be able to write some kind of artist statement explaining their creative process; film studies majors have writing and analysis requirements; and the list goes on. Much of what we do in courses like this could be presented at campus, regional, national, or international conferences, because it represents the discovery of knowledge. See the upper-division film seminar *FILM 301: Issues in Lens-Based Media* and its learning outcomes in the preface. *FILM 301* is one of the most challenging courses, both in terms of creative thinking and final product expectations, in the

School of Film & Photography's new BFA program in Integrated Lens-Based Media at MSU.

How to Use This Text

Although intended as a text for junior and senior film studies courses, this text can fulfill other functions. It should be an interesting read for all film majors, whatever their particular focus, and it can also be used as a reference for particular subject areas. The sample abstracts at the end of the topic chapters are just a beginning, there are many more online and in print. This text might also give students and faculty members ideas about other things they can organize to increase the visibility and activity on their own campuses with respect to undergraduate research in film.

Conclusion

As film majors increasingly participate in undergraduate research and become familiar with that term as an umbrella term for many of the creative and scholarly activities they pursue, film degrees will become more challenging yet more engaging and fun. The filmmaking process itself will be viewed more as a scholarly activity by people in other disciplines and less as mere entertainment.

Questions for Discussion

- What is the difference between creativity in science and creativity in film?
- How do the terms inquiry, creativity, scholarship, and research differ?
- Why do employers prefer students who have done undergraduate research?
- Do all film professors do research, and how much do they need to do?

References

Anderson, W. (2012). Creating a singular "kingdom" (May 29). NPR. Retrieved from https://www.npr.org/2012/05/29/153913922/wes-anderson-creating-a-singular-kingdom.

Council on Undergraduate Research. (2016). Learning through research. Retrieved from www.cur.org.

Digital Storytelling Multimedia Archive. (2012). Using images in digital storytelling. Retrieved from https://pilot.cndls.georgetown.edu/digitalstories/multimedia-distinctive/2/2/.

Egan, K. (1989). *Teaching as storytelling*. Chicago, IL: The University of Chicago Press.

Osborn, J. M. & Karukstis, K. K. (2009). The benefits of undergraduate research, scholarship, and creative activity. In M. Boyd and J. Wesemann (Eds.), *Broadening participation in undergraduate research: Fostering excellence and enhancing the impact* (pp. 41–53). Washington, DC: Council on Undergraduate Research.

Stanton, C. R., Hall, B., & Ricciardelli, L. (2017). Cross-cultural digital storywork: A framework for engagement with/in indigenous communities. *Engaged Scholar Journal: Community-Engaged Research, Teaching, and Learning, 2*(1): 247–266.

Stanton, C. R., Ricciardelli, L., & Hall, B. (2017). Re-visioning self-determination: Planning for culturally sustaining/revitalizing oral histories with indigenous communities. In K. Llewellyn and N. Ng-A-Fook (Eds.), *Oral history and education* (pp. 207–230). London: Palgrave Macmillan.

2

LITERATURE REVIEWS

> The difference between literature and journalism is that journalism is unreadable, and literature is not read.
>
> Oscar Wilde

> Literature is an investment of genius which has dividends to all subsequent times.
>
> John Burroughs

Summary

A literature review is an organized, informed discussion of published works that are significant to the subject of study, in this case, the study of film. It conveys the relationship between the present study and what has already been published in the field. By reviewing the literature, scholars join important conversations in the discipline of film, with critical understanding of what others have said, how the voices in the conversation relate to one another, and where they might add insight.

Purpose and Format of a Literature Review

Conducting research on film and reporting on its results is a professional way of joining a vibrant, ongoing conversation about the field. Contributing to that interesting conversation entails understanding what others have said, how the voices in the conversation relate to one another, and where further insight might be added. To contribute meaningfully to the conversation, scholars need to study published material, the "literature," related to the topic. Much like other reviews, a literature review is an analysis of that published material.

A literature review provides context for your research study by explaining what is already known and what needs further exploration. In doing so, it establishes your credibility as a researcher, demonstrating that your project or study did not emerge from "out of the blue," but from thoughtful consideration of what has been published already and how your work fits in to that framework. The literature review should accomplish three main objectives:

1. Briefly summarize the salient points of the most important publications on the topic of study.
2. Explain the relationships among those published works (e.g., how a major study changed the field, why some scholars came to differing conclusions on a key question, how the introduction of a new factor or variable in one study led to surprising results).
3. Identify gaps in the literature—the questions or issues that have not yet been examined.

By identifying gaps in the research literature, this third objective is critical to showing the need for your study. The literature review shows that you have read and analyzed important sources on the topic, and at least one significant question has not been addressed or has not been definitively answered. That is the gap your study seeks to fill.

Literature Review versus Annotated Bibliography

The format of a literature review is different from that of an annotated bibliography, which summarizes or describes one source after another in a few sentences each. If your professor assigns an annotated bibliography as well as a literature review for your research project, you would complete the annotated bibliography first, as it represents your first pass through the relevant literature. Although annotated bibliographies usually include a brief evaluation of each source, each entry is its own individual item, listed in alphabetical order by author last name. The bibliography entries do not connect with each other except for the fact that they are on the same general topic. A literature review, however, is not in a list; it is a narrative that could stand on its own as a coherent essay, with unified paragraphs and transitions between points. Your literature review allows you to "tell the story" of what scholars already understand about the topic and how they have informed your own study. Specific strategies for organizing your literature review are laid out later in this chapter.

Joining a Scholarly Conversation

Almost everyone has had the irritating experience of being interrupted from what had been an interesting conversation by someone who does not know what has already been said but jumps in with opinions anyway. Sometimes the interrupter spouts unrelated ideas or rehashes a point from which the conversation has already moved on. The interrupter, in such cases, shows disrespect to the people who have already been engaged in the conversation as well as a lack of credibility. The group would probably dismiss the interrupter's ideas, even if they are potentially good ones, because they appear to be random and uninformed. For good reason, most of us have been socialized to join an ongoing conversation in a more respectful way: only after listening for a little while and gaining familiarity with the topic. A new person joining a conversation should ask or wait to hear what the group is talking about or allow someone already involved in the conversation to offer a recap.

That metaphor of *joining an ongoing conversation* is a useful way of thinking about a literature review. A "conversation" about the topic (or closely related to the topic) has been going on in the field, as represented in the published research literature. Reading the literature allows new scholars in the field to listen to what has been said and join the conversation as informed participants. Only by closely reading, or "listening" to, the previous participants' ideas can you contribute something original and interesting to the conversation, such as a new idea that has not been completely covered already or a question about someone else's point that adds an intriguing dimension to the topic. In other words, by conducting a review of the research literature you avoid "interrupting" a conversation with stale opinions or irrelevant questions; instead, you can knowledgeably participate in a discussion of an interesting topic with a group of scholars who also deeply care about it.

Finding Appropriate Sources

Peer-Reviewed Sources

For most scholarly projects in film, the literature review will be based on *peer-reviewed sources*. Peer review is a process of quality control to ensure that articles and books accepted for publication are accurate and based on valid research methods. Academic journals and book publishers typically rely on rigorous peer-review processes before publishing someone's research. To be considered for publication, a researcher submits an article or chapter to an editor, who reaches out to experts specializing in the author's area of study to ask them to review it. Those experts are the researcher's "peers." Most peer reviews are *double-blind*, meaning that the researcher does not know who is reviewing the work, and reviewers do not know who authored it. Whether they are reviewing "blindly" or not, the reviewers are expected to evaluate the quality of the work impartially. They use their own expertise to determine whether the author conducted a valid and reliable research study, whether the findings or conclusions are sound, and to what degree the research makes an important contribution to the field of study. Peer reviewers usually can accept a work "as is" (perhaps with minor edits) or "with revision" (requiring the author to address particular questions or problems in the next draft). Otherwise, if the work does not meet the standards for research in the discipline, the reviewers reject it. Due to a rigorous process of review that determines whether a work is published or not, peer-reviewed journal articles and books are considered the best quality scholarship. On the spectrum of reliable sources of information, one might think of peer-reviewed articles as opposite to "fake news" on social media. Any information simply made up by the author would be rejected by peer reviewers, who demand evidence of careful methods and accurate reporting. The professional reputations of a journal's or publisher's peer reviewers are as much on the line as those of the authors being published.

This book, for example, went through two peer-review processes. This book began, as most do, as a proposal submitted to a publisher. The proposal included an explanation of the need we saw for such a book, a proposed outline of chapters with brief descriptions of what would be included in each, and a sample chapter. The publisher forwarded the proposal to three experts in the field: film professors at different universities who mentor undergraduate research and have presented at conferences and/or published on the topic of Undergraduate Research in Film—in other words, the reviewers were our peers. The peer reviewers each made recommendations about additional topics for us to include and other sources for us to consult, and they each recommended to the publisher that we proceed with writing the book. Once a full draft (a *manuscript*) was complete, it went through a different round of peer review, through which we received additional revision suggestions that made the final product considerably stronger.

If a professor or editor asks for a literature review of *peer-reviewed sources*, this is why: only high-quality research studies will inform the work. Researchers are unlikely to be led astray by false or unverified information when they stick to peer-reviewed journals and books. That said, it is sometimes acceptable to include non-peer-reviewed sources in a literature review, especially if the sources can be verified as reliable through other means (more about that later in this chapter) and/or if the topic of study has not received much attention yet from academic scholars. Consider, for example, a literature review on a contemporary filmmaker or an emerging film genre. Because the peer-review process takes time, academic articles and books are published many months after the manuscripts are first submitted. Experts in the film industry, however, may be able to publish informative articles in a popular press in a matter of days. A film review or analysis published in *The New Yorker* is not a peer-reviewed scholarly piece, but it is reliable and therefore may be a valuable part of a literature review.

Library Databases

The best place to find peer-reviewed, scholarly articles is in online databases to which your college or university library subscribes. Starting with open-source repositories of scholarship such as Google Scholar is fine, but most academic journal articles are still found in subscription-only databases such as Academic Search Premier, EBSCOhost, JSTOR, and, for the purposes of film research, Film and Television Literature Index, Academic Video Online (AVON), Alexander Street Press Video, Filmakers Library Online Video and PBS Video Collection, among others. We recommend consulting with a reference librarian to learn about the relevant online databases for your topic area and how to access them. Many college/university library websites offer online tutorials for using databases. If you prefer a tutorial in person, a reference librarian may be able to walk you through the basic guidelines for the databases to which the library is subscribed. Knowing the specific parameters for searching each database (e.g., which truncation symbols and Boolean operators it recognizes) helps make searches more efficient and effective. Truncation symbols allow users to search for multiple, closely related words at one time. Some databases use # as a truncation symbol, while others use * (e.g., educa# for educate, education, educator, and educational; or wom*n for woman and women). Boolean operators are conjunctions (e.g., *and, or*) and other connecting words (e.g., *not*) that are used to include or exclude certain terms from a search. For example, a search for information about contemporary American director Wes Anderson might use Boolean operators in this way: Wes AND Anderson AND filmmaker NOT Paul Thomas (to exclude contemporary American director Paul Thomas Anderson). Another option for that search in many databases is "Wes Anderson," indicating that only results with *Wes* and *Anderson* adjacent to one another will be found. A few databases, though, use single quotation marks for that purpose ('Wes Anderson') and still others do not use quotation marks at all to keep terms together! Until the unlikely day when all database builders will agree on a single system, consulting a reference librarian or a written guide to library databases is essential to finding the right information.

In order to identify relevant books and articles, researchers use a variety of search terms. To yield comprehensive results, reference librarians sometimes recommend making a list of alternative terms and subjects related to your topic area and then conducting database searches using all of those terms. When researchers have trouble locating information, the problem is often that they have not hit upon the precise search terms used in the database. For example, someone researching *Canadian documentary filmmakers* may find that using the terms *North American* and *director* will yield additional results.

Experienced scholars know that the bibliographies of sources already found are excellent resources for identifying additional sources. By reading the titles of books, articles, or films (and the names of journals in which they appear) in bibliographies, researchers can find a rich trove of additional texts to read and films to watch. If the same source is referenced repeatedly, that is a good indication of its importance in the field. Similarly, when scholars find a particularly useful source, they search to discover what else the author has written and whether the journal has published any similar articles.

Analyzing Existing Research in Film

In addition to being called "literature," the articles located through database searches are often referred to as *existing research* to differentiate those works from the original research you are conducting in your own study. Articles and books are also called *secondary sources* as a way of contrasting them from the *primary sources* that some studies utilize, such as a filmmaker's diaries, letters, notebooks, interviews, scripts, and shooting schedules. Secondary sources are articles and books that analyze (a) other texts (film scripts, production notes, storyboards, historical or legal documents, and other primary sources), (b) recordings (audio and/or video), (c) historical events and eras, (d) statistical or experimental data, or (e) people's lives, words, or actions.

To do the analysis required for a literature review, we recommend printing hard copies of articles and reading them with a pencil in hand, ready to underline sentences, circle key words, and take notes in the margins. When reading digital copies of articles or library copies of books, using a research journal (a spiral notebook is perfect) can substitute well for writing on a hard copy. Using a form of shorthand that at least you can understand later, you can make note of important points, key terms, and questions that arise as you read. That kind of critical reflection is the vital piece missing from inadequate literature reviews. Giving time and consideration to reflect on and position yourself in dialogue with the sources yields a much more nuanced and resonant study than the so-called "research sausage" that is created by throwing together a little from this article, a little from that book, etc. and trying to fit it all into the preformed casing of a "literature review."

Reading Reflectively

The following suggestions are a guide for reflective reading of articles in preparation for a literature review.

1. *Read the Abstract first, then the Conclusion, before starting the body of the article.* That strategy allows you to determine the relevance of the article to the study and, if it is indeed relevant, to boost your comprehension of its main ideas. After reading the Abstract and Conclusion, skim the section headings and subheadings, and look at any figures or graphs. Then begin reading with the end in mind. A clearer sense of the relative importance

of each paragraph to the overall article becomes evident, allowing you to know which paragraphs can be skimmed and which need focused attention.

2. *The "halo effect"* is a cognitive bias that, in this situation, can lead a reader to assume that because an author's work is published in a peer-reviewed journal, the author must be "right," even though research is rarely definitive. As careful researchers read, they keep their mind open to various perspectives on the topic by alternately accepting the author's viewpoint and then raising questions about the research methods, limitations of the study, strength of the evidence, and the conclusions that are drawn. By following that model and raising questions and identifying the limitations as you read, you will help yourself in two ways: you will be able to draw more interesting and nuanced connections between sources in the literature review when you notice how each argument is constructed, and your analysis could lead to discovery of a "gap" in the research.
3. *Approach reading as a multiple-draft process*, not unlike the writing process. Scholars reread some parts of each article, deepening their understanding with each return to the text. Academic writing, in particular, is densely constructed and written for experts in the field. It demands more than a single-shot reading to grasp its meaning and implications. Anyone new to reading and analyzing research literature is likely to feel lost in the complex sentence structures and specialized terminology. It is written that way not to confuse readers but to convey as efficiently as possible very sophisticated ideas to a highly educated audience. A metaphor we use with our students is that of a tightly packed suitcase: it took a great deal of planning and care for the author to use the space efficiently; as you "unpack" it you may need to move slowly, examining one item or point at a time, noting its significance before moving to the next.
4. *Continually ask how each article or book chapter relates to the topic area being explored.* Could it help contextualize the problem? Does it show that your research question remains unanswered? Does it demonstrate how other scholars have attempted to address the question differently than your study will? In this way you can begin painless drafting of other parts of the research paper; for example, an article that corroborates the identified problem can be referenced in the introduction.
5. *Learn the context for each source.* Where does it appear (if an article)? What other kinds of articles does that journal publish? When was it written? Have there been more recent and/or more important publications on the matter? (The importance of an article can be determined in part by noting how often it is cited in other articles.) If it is an article that appears on a website or in a periodical that is not peer-reviewed, how reliable/credible is the source? (See the "credibility check" at the end of this section.) If the source is a book, what can be determined about the publisher? A university press indicates a peer-reviewed, academic source. Other

publishers, such as the press that produced this book (Routledge), can be looked up easily in order to discover what other kinds of texts they publish.

6. *Throughout this process, take thorough notes.* When reading hard copies, we ditch the highlighter in favor of a pencil. Underlining points, circling key terms, and writing margin notes are more active tasks than highlighting. Interacting directly with the text on the page helps with retention of information, more thoughtful use of the material, and more sophisticated insights. When using digital sources or library books, take notes, with page and paragraph numbers, in a reading journal. That is helpful not only for efficiently referring back to sources, but also for keeping track of your thinking on a topic over time and how it evolves with each new piece of information. One strategy for fruitful note-taking is to write down what was most exciting, convincing, doubtful, and/or confusing about each article or book chapter, as well as what questions it raised. Engaging with the text and asking questions about it are essential aspects of joining the community of scholars in the field.
7. *Keep meticulous records of bibliographic information* (author, article title, journal title, name of the database, date of publication, date of access, and page numbers) in the research journal. Most of that information can be cut and pasted right into a draft bibliography. As too many of us know, unearthing that information later is frustrating work!
8. *Learn the citation style expected for the literature review and use it in all notes and drafts.* Whereas humanities scholars usually use MLA (Modern Language Association) style, scholars of art history adopt Chicago or Turabian (a variation of Chicago) style, and film journalists utilize AP (Associated Press) or APA (American Psychological Association). Getting into the practice of citing the research sources in the correct form from the very beginning will save you time in reformatting later, as well as instill the citation rules in a hands-on, timely manner.

Checking the Credibility of Sources

Conduct a *credibility check* on the research sources that are not from peer-reviewed journals or book publishers. You should be able to answer "yes" to the following questions:

- Is the article free of errors in spelling and grammar? Do the vocabulary and sentence structures seem appropriate for academic research purposes?
- Is the author or sponsoring organization identified? Is the author qualified? Is the author affiliated with an accredited university, a nonprofit organization, or a government agency? (Qualifications and affiliations should be clearly identifiable.)

- Is there documentation for the information provided, in citations and a bibliography?
- Is the information verifiable in other sources?
- If the article is from a website, can the purpose of the site be determined (e.g., nonprofit advocacy, business/marketing, objective information/reference, for-profit news, personal soapbox)? Is that purpose seemingly impartial? (In other words, it should not be overtly trying to sway readers to a particular opinion or to purchase a product.)
- Does it include a publication date or "last updated" date? Is it current?
- If a website or blog, does it contain its own substantive content, as opposed to mainly providing links to other sites?
- Are links accurately described and still working?

Organizing the Content of a Literature Review

As stated at the beginning of this chapter, a literature review is an *organized* discussion of published works. It does not follow the order in which the researcher found or read each source; that would be a reading journal—not particularly helpful to anyone besides the researcher. And literature reviews are rarely organized in chronological order, beginning with the oldest publication and moving forward in time or beginning with the most recent and moving backward. It only makes sense to organize a literature review chronologically when showing the changing trends in the area of study is critical to your research. For example, a study examining what is the most popular editing software used in American academic film programs in 2019 may need to examine the evolution of film editing since the emergence of digital technology or how the transition from analog to digital has affected editing practices in the United States. In such a case, a researcher could simply order the literature review from the oldest research to the most recent (or vice versa, as the case demands) and make clear that the sequential development is critical to one's understanding of the issue.

Most literature reviews are organized *thematically*, around a few main ideas. Strong transitions between each main idea show how one relates to another, such as how new methods evolved from previous ones or how scholars in different parts of the world or from different schools of thought pursued similar questions in markedly distinct ways. How does one (a) identify a few main ideas from many disparate sources and (b) create transitions between them when they appear to be only loosely related? The strategy for accomplishing both of those complex tasks is to start grouping sources—and, usually, parts of different sources—at the time of reading. We recommend starting with big categories of the matters most often discussed in literature reviews: methods, findings, implications, and key characteristics of studies (anything in addition to the main methods, findings, and implications that stands out, such as a national study conducted in a very small country or the timing of data collection immediately after a major event that could reasonably be thought to influence results).

Organizing in a Table or Spreadsheet

As experienced researchers read and take notes on the literature, they also start to organize their sources, such as in a table or spreadsheet, which helps with subsequent tracking of patterns and relationships among the sources. See Table 2.1 for an example of a table you might use to jot down salient elements of a few sources.

By jotting down key characteristics, methods, findings, and implications of each source, you can identify noteworthy contrasts as well as similarities. For example, the two or three sources that used *mixed methods* (a mixture of qualitative and quantitative methods, which is explained in Chapter 5), when most other published research on the topic has relied on quantitative data exclusively, could be discussed together in the literature review. Or, studies that came to vastly different conclusions could be juxtaposed for contrast.

Organizing in Narrative Form or Bullet Points

Some researchers prefer writing notes about each source in narrative form or in bullet points and then coding their notes for themes, patterns, and key differences. *Coding* in this instance refers to using different color highlights and/or different symbols (e.g., double underlining, asterisks) to mark patterns in a set of notes. For example, every mention of study subjects who are young children is highlighted yellow, while every mention of subjects who are adolescents is highlighted green. Or opposing findings are marked with left and right brackets (<, >). The following questions may serve as prompts for the narrative or bulleted notes for each source:

- Is the significance of the author's work convincingly demonstrated?
- What are the author's theoretical approaches and/or research methods?

TABLE 2.1 Literature review table

Authors	*Publication date*	*Key characteristics of the study*	*Methods*	*Findings*	*Implications & my evaluation*

- What are strengths and/or limitations of the author's research methods?
- Was the study designed well?
- What are the main findings and their implications?
- Are the author's analysis and conclusions convincing?
- In what ways does the author's work contribute to the field of study?
- What are the article's or book's overall strengths and limitations?
- How does the work relate to your study?

Moving from Notes to Draft

Whether in a table, highlighted jottings, annotated bullet points, or other format, your organized notes about the research literature will help lead to the identification of patterns or other categories of information, known as *themes*. Each of the themes that emerge can become a paragraph or series of paragraphs of the literature review. Organizing the discussion of the research literature by themes highlights connections among the works under review. Such organization also demonstrates to the audience that you have conducted reflective and thoughtful research that has led to intriguing insights. For it is your organized evaluation and analysis of the various sources' methods, evidence, findings, limitations, etc. that will give the literature review shape as an interesting argument. You will bring the research literature to life, so to speak, by moving well beyond summarizing key studies and even beyond noting some patterns. By organizing the literature review and choosing which sources to group with which and explaining how sources evolve from and/or dispute one another, you can make a unique set of claims about the literature on your topic of inquiry.

A well-organized, analytical literature review sets the stage for what comes next: the research questions to be examined in your study. For that reason, the conclusion of the literature review is the most important part. The last paragraph establishes where the existing literature leaves off and the present research proceeds. It demonstrates the need for the present study and what it will contribute to current knowledge.

Questions for Discussion

- Is a literature review important for all academic projects?
- How do literature reviews vary by subject area?
- How do you know if your literature review is sufficient?

References

Burroughs, J. (2016). *Indoor studies*. Charleston, SC: BiblioLife LLC. Original work published 1895.

Wilde, O. (2007). *The critic as artist*. New York: Mondial. Original work published 1891.

3

CHOOSING FILM TOPICS AND FORMULATING APPROPRIATE RESEARCH QUESTIONS

> The practical man is the adventurer, the investigator, the believer in research, the asker of questions, the man who refuses to believe that perfection has been attained ... There is no thrill or joy in merely doing that which any one can do ... It is always safe to assume, not that the old way is wrong, but that there may be a better way.
>
> Henry R. Harrower

Summary

This chapter discusses the importance of formulating research questions that are unanswered, yet answerable, and the processes that could be used to address them. It is essential that the development of research questions and refining of a research topic occur after, and are informed by, a thorough literature review. Frequently, undergraduate students' initial suggestions for film research topics tend to be either much too broad or too narrow in scope, and a literature review would quickly reveal this. If a question can be answered with a simple "yes" or "no" answer, it isn't appropriate for a research study. When formulating a research question, it is advisable that film students communicate with a professor outside of their discipline, who can offer a different perspective. Such co-mentorship broadens the base of expertise from which students can draw.

Brainstorming Topic Areas

In order to generate ideas for a topic of research that is focused, timely, and of keen interest in your field of study, brainstorm responses to the following questions:

- What are some interesting topics of conversation among you and your friends that relate to being a filmmaker, studying film for your major, and/or pursuing a career in film?
- On the other hand, what topics rarely discussed by your friends seem significant to you?
- Are there any trends in the technology or practice of film that you have embraced or resisted?
- Do you disagree with the "conventional wisdom" on a particular philosophy, practice, or stance in the field of filmmaking?
- Have you recently come to value something in your studies that had not previously seemed important to you?
- Where are many people in your field of study going wrong (in your humble opinion)?
- What are you most interested in learning about or contributing to in your intended career?

Refining the Topic

Starting with a broad topic area when embarking on a research study is common and perfectly acceptable. You might begin with general interest in an area of study, such as how digital technology is affecting traditional linear storytelling, what makes Quentin Tarantino so popular among undergraduate film students, or why there is a decline of 3-D box office sales. You might even think that if you are taking on a long-term research project of a whole semester or more you will need a large topic to sustain the work all that time. Ironically, however, the opposite is usually true. A significant, long-term research study requires a specific, focused question. Getting the scope of that question right is the most valuable task to accomplish early in the research process.

The preliminary research and brainstorming you put into refining the topic are well worthwhile because, as we and our colleagues have seen repeatedly with our students' research (not to mention our own scholarly work!), the scope of the question can make or break the project. Imagine trying to carry out a comprehensive study of how digital technology is affecting traditional chronological narrative structures by giving rise to interactive storytelling (Lanham, 1994). Within that broad topic area there are dozens of possible approaches. For example, would it be a study about the logic of the hypertext and its impact on linear thinking? Would it be a technological and historical exploration of interactive storytelling environments? And what is even meant by "interactive storytelling"? Is it simply a form of digital entertainment? Or rather, is it a sophisticated multimedia system that gives computer users agency in the way a story is generated?

As would be the case for that interactive storytelling example, topics that are too broad can cause frustration and lead to wasted time. If it turned out you were most interested in exploring the logic of the hypertext and its impact on linear reasoning, you would likely be reading some postmodern theories about the influence of digital technology on Eurocentric knowledge, rather than, say, studying what type of algorithms form the foundation of interactive storytelling and how they work. Each of those approaches is significant and time intensive in its own right. Skipping around multiple areas of a broad topic area results in a shallow and/or chaotic exploration. The clearer your focus, the more efficiently you can use your time and resources to conduct an in-depth, well-informed study.

Using the Literature Review and Plenty of Time to Focus the Question

Your review of the literature, as well as conversations with your professors, peers, and perhaps external experts, will allow you to understand what others have said about the topic and, in the process, help focus and refine your area of inquiry. By posing questions, analyzing the problem, and imagining various solutions, you will come to a deeper, more thorough comprehension of what is at issue and how to address it most effectively. This period of refining the topic into a strong, focused research question will be most valuable and satisfying if you give yourself adequate time and reflective space, as well as permission to scrap some ideas and begin again.

Very few scholars arrive at a perfectly refined research question through a singular epiphany. Most of us, most of the time, have to wallow around in half-formed ideas, mistaken directions, and—most frustrating of all—pursuits that have to abandoned after days or even weeks of seemingly wasted work. Rather than fearing or trying to avoid "wasted" time—and, as a result, ending up with a simplistic or otherwise ineffectual project—try to see this time as an essential and valuable part of the process of creatively and comprehensively addressing a complex issue. If you are truly confronting a focused, significant, and problematic question—one with no single, agreed-upon solution—you will need to invest in a few good stumbling-around periods.

Guiding Questions for Refining a Topic

Taking time for focusing and refining your question does not need to be wasted time; in fact, it can be time incalculably well spent, particularly if you are engaging some critical, foundational questions:

- Why is the topic or question important? To whom is it important? Are particular groups of people affected more than others?
- What gives the topic tension? What would draw readers to learning more about it?

- Read at least five current (i.e., usually published in the last five years) research articles about your topic and imagine yourself as a participant in a dialogue with the authors of the articles. What are the questions you would ask them? What seems to be missing or undervalued?
- What are the sources of the problem or question? Complex questions usually have complex webs of potential causes. Can you identify some of the strands of that web? Do you know professors or outside experts who can help?
- What is the history or broader context of the topic? To get a handle on the context of your topic area, use reliable, general resources available through many college and university library websites and physical holdings, such as *Oxford Scholarship Online: Film Theory and Philosophy*, *The Film Encyclopedia 7th Edition: The Complete Guide to Film and the Film Industry*, or *Film Histories: An Introduction and Reader*, which includes large sections on social and cultural dimensions of film history and exposes film students to different forms of historical research and topics, from the history of exhibition practices, to censorship, film aesthetic, film politics and audience reception.
- What other subject areas is your topic part of or related to? Might those other areas provide additional perspectives and/or interdisciplinary possibilities for research?
- Why do you care about the topic area? What is its connection to your personal experiences or interests? In what ways does the interest extend beyond yourself, to other scholars and professionals in the field?
- Who is the principal audience you want to reach with your research results? What do you want the audience to do as a result of your research: Adjust their thinking about the issue? Change some aspect of their practices/work/activities? Provide support (e.g., funding, advocacy)? Experience something new?

Freewriting

Write down your responses to these questions and other ideas that come to you. Writing is the best way to reach clarity and insight about the issue you are exploring. Instead of trying to brainstorm only in your mind, we strongly recommend putting pen to paper or fingers to keyboard and *freewriting* your ideas for at least ten minutes at a time. Do not suppress any ideas even if they seem flawed, and do not do any editing for correctness. The kinesthetic act of writing (moving a pen across paper or typing on a keyboard), along with the mental "unblocking" of ideas, leads to insights that simply do not arrive if you stare at a blank screen or piece of paper. Freewriting is a wonderfully simple and highly effective means of getting past "writer's block" or just getting off the "starting block" of any writing task.

Professor Peter Elbow (1973), who has defined the drafting and revision process for college students for decades, explains the process of freewriting in his classic 1973 text *Writing without Teachers*:

> The idea is simply to write for ten minutes (later on, perhaps fifteen or twenty). Don't stop for anything. Go quickly without rushing. Never stop to look back, to cross something out … to wonder what word or thought to use, or to think about what you are doing. If you can't think of a word or a spelling, just use a squiggle or else write, "I can't think of it." Just put down something.
>
> *(p. 1)*

Freewriting allows you to get past your own internal critic and tap into subconscious, creative ideas that are difficult to access any other way (Boice, 1993). Such active brainstorming will produce a lot of material—plenty to throw out eventually, but also some rich ore that you may not have uncovered without journaling. The added bonus: you have notes for writing a first draft later. Even decades into our academic careers we use this freewriting strategy at the outset of new projects and when writer's block hits. Something almost magical often occurs at about the ten-minute mark of freewriting: a breakthrough of an exciting idea, more clarity about a muddled topic, or the concept for a new and better direction.

Topic Areas in Film

Undergraduate research in film often takes the form of one of the following broad areas. (Many more possible topics can be found in Chapters 9–17.)

1. *Film History*
   Examples: *the filmic construction of national identity in early European cinema (1890s–1919); is the Italian "spaghetti western" a transnational genre?; the historical development of special effects technologies in cinema from Georges Méliès to James Cameron.*
2. *Film Education*
   Examples: *how emerging technologies are influencing students' audiovisual perceptions; how outreach programs involving the teaching of filmmaking skills can benefit middle-school students as well as their college-student mentors.*
3. *Film from an Interdisciplinary Perspective*
   Examples: *research technological innovations in film equipment that have been inspired from biology; apply indigenous methodologies to the study of Hollywood-inspired storytelling approaches.*
4. *Film Theory*
   Examples: *postmodern documentary filmmaking and its blurring of the boundaries between fiction and nonfiction; investigate some of the ways in which film theory informs film production.*

5. *Film Technology*
   Examples: *investigate how mobile technology has affected contemporary film-making production; analyze film reception in the digital age (e.g., computer screen and mobile screen as an alternative to movie theaters' screens).*

As each of the examples indicates, undergraduate research in film invites you to explore something different from what has been done in the past. It absolutely should be something uncertain, risky, or challenging—something that takes you from familiar practices and assumptions to new and surprising ones. Of course, trying something uncertain, risky, or challenging can be daunting and uncomfortable, but it is essential to an interesting and purposeful study.

Designing a Research Study or Project

Investing time in focusing and refining your topic of inquiry undoubtedly helped you revise your research question. You are ready to develop and carry out your research plan, including creating a timeframe and figuring out logistics.

Will you be working with human participants in your research? Will you be distributing a survey, conducting interviews or focus-group discussions, recruiting volunteers or asking people to try a particular intervention? If your answer is yes to any of those questions, or if you are otherwise interacting with people online or in person (other than your professors or librarians) for any part of your research, you need approval or exemption from your university's Institutional Review Board (IRB). See Chapter 4 about research involving human participants. In the meantime, for the sake of planning your research, be sure to build in time to write an IRB application, have it reviewed, and to make any amendments to your research that the IRB could require.

Freewrite/brainstorm responses to the following questions to help you design your plan:

1. If people will be involved in your research (survey-takers, interviewees, etc.), what is your goal for the "sample size" (number of people to recruit)? What are their key characteristics (e.g., college students majoring in STEM, adults who learned to edit footage after age 20, fans of a particular film genre)? How will you recruit the participants you need? How will you reduce bias in your sample?
2. How will your study be different from what has been done by previous scholars (especially if it is similar to research in the literature)?
3. How does your study reflect "best practices" in the field, promote diversity and inclusion, and engage with timely and significant matters?
4. Is your research question large enough that it should be broken into two or three parts? "Unpacking" a research question into two or more stages or facets of the research can help organize your timeline as well as your

eventual research paper. For example, assessing the effectiveness of a community film outreach program could involve the following facets: (a) surveys of the people on the receiving end; (b) interviews with the organizers; (c) focus groups with the people providing the service. Each could be written up separately, followed by a summation paper bringing all three together.

Organizing a Timeline

Such brainstorming and figuring out the parts of your research design can lead to the creation of an organized timeline. Table 3.1 is set up for a semester research essay (whether written or audiovisual). Of course, yours should account for the time you have for your particular study. Keep adding to it as you realize additional facets of the project.

Purpose Statements

In many forms of academic research, scholars state the purpose of their study or project in one or two sentences. Stating directly and succinctly the purpose of your study clarifies it for yourself at the outset, as well as for your future readers. After the purpose statement, state the research question or questions that will be guiding your study.

Example 1: *The purpose of this study is to …*
Guiding the design of this study are the following questions:
Example 2: *This research project examines …*
The following questions determined the focus of the research:

Briefly articulating your study's purpose and identifying a manageable number of research questions can keep you on task. Write down your purpose and most critical research questions and post them at your work space. Just

TABLE 3.1 Timeline table

What do I need to do in the next week?	*1–2 weeks from now (dates: ____)*	*3–4 weeks from now (dates: ____)*	*1–2 months from now (dates: ____)*	*3–4 months from now (dates: ____)*

about any research study can easily mushroom into an overly ambitious project, particularly if you are doing a good job of reading related literature and considering multiple perspectives. Having the parameters of your study posted right in front of you may help you resist the temptation to totalize—to take on more than you can reasonably investigate, at least for now, in the attempt to be comprehensive.

Additional Mentors

Especially in film, there are many specialty areas and sub-disciplines in which different professors have expertise (animation, documentary filmmaking, interactive storytelling, critical theory, history, theater, music, computer science, education, etc.). Therefore, students can usually find certain professors who have an interest in the topic they are planning to research. Even if professors with the right expertise are not your instructors, one of them might be interested enough in the topic to be an additional mentor, or might have a research project already in progress that could benefit from the assistance of an undergraduate researcher.

Interdisciplinary student projects particularly lend themselves to more than one faculty mentor. *Interdisciplinary* describes work that emerges from more than one academic discipline's knowledge base, research methods, ways of knowing (or *epistemologies*), and scholarly values. The two or more disciplines shape the work together, resulting in an approach and findings that could not be achieved through a single disciplinary perspective. Consider, for example, the interdisciplinary connection between the fields of film and biology; for research in those areas, students may need expert guidance not only from film instructors but also from biology professors. One of the examples of interdisciplinary research topics in film provided above, *research technological innovations in film equipment that have been inspired from biology*, came from a student project that was co-mentored by me (Ricciardelli) and a faculty professor in the biology department. His expertise, as well as his access to research findings, was essential to the study.

Will Success Be Measurable?

The ways to measure success will vary greatly depending on the particular topic, but some components of research success include whether or not the project allows you to make an *original discovery* of something you and your mentor did not fully expect to find; whether some *new knowledge* is created, even if that knowledge is different from the anticipated results; and if the findings indicate an *advancement of the discipline*, even in a small way. Successful dissemination of results, covered in depth in Chapter 8 of this book, is also a measure of success. Dissemination could be through a presentation or publication, or both.

Questions for Discussion

- How do I know when I have a good research question?
- When do I have to be sure of my topic and my research question?
- What should be on the checklist for choosing a topic/question?

References

Boice, R. (1993). Writing blocks and tacit knowledge. *The Journal of Higher Education, 64* (1): 19–54.

Elbow, P. (1973). *Writing without teachers*. New York: Oxford University Press.

Harrower, H. R. (n.d.). Retrieved from www.azquotes.com/quote/614665.

Lanham, R. (1994). The implications of electronic information for the sociology of knowledge. *Leonardo, 27*(2): 156.

4

WORKING WITH HUMAN SUBJECTS

> Genetically speaking, humans are terrible research subjects. We're genetically promiscuous—we mate with anyone we choose—and we don't take kindly to scientists telling us who we should reproduce with. Plus, unlike plants and mice, it takes decades to produce enough offspring to give scientists much meaningful data.
>
> Rebecca Skloot

> Research is formalized curiosity. It is poking and prying with a purpose.
>
> Zora Neale Hurston

Summary

The focus of this chapter is Human Subjects Research. We define and discuss the role of the university Institutional Review Board (IRB) in reviewing, approving, and monitoring research involving human subjects, or human participants, in order to ensure that all research is conducted in accordance with federal, institutional, and ethical guidelines. We provide an overview of the Collaborative Institutional Training Initiative (CITI), including information for students about what to expect and a rationale for participating in the training. A brief synopsis of Rebecca Skloot's book, *The Immortal Life of Henrietta Lacks*, is included as a means of illustrating the far-reaching effects of unethical research methods, even when the researcher is well intentioned. The chapter concludes with a brief overview of types of film projects requiring IRB approval and CITI training.

Human Subjects Research

Any type of research that involves people—people who take a survey, people who are interviewed, people who participate in an experiment or study, etc.—is *human subjects research* or *human participants research*. A particular group of humans—what they think, how they change, what they do—is a subject of the research. Even if a very small part of the research includes people, even if the people are minimally consulted, and/or even if only one or two people are affected, the rules of *human subjects research* apply.

Human Subjects or Human Participants?

The traditional term *human subjects* is still used in most training programs and US federal guidelines, including those governing research conducted by the Department of Health and Human Services. Since the 1980s, though, largely due to the work of those engaged in research into the AIDS epidemic, the term *human participants* has often been used to refer to the people involved in a research study of any kind (Bayer, 1995). When AIDS was first identified, those who had contracted the disease, especially gay men and people who had used intravenous drugs, were acutely vulnerable to social stigma as well as incarceration. Homosexuality was considered a crime in over half of the states in the US, was a disqualifier for teaching jobs and military service and was often used as grounds for taking away parental rights. AIDS researchers needed to take thorough care not only to protect identifying information of patients, but also to ask questions with keen sensitivity and without apparent judgment regarding patients' sexuality or drug use.

> In a remarkable and quite unusual process, all the more striking since it occurred during the conservative Reagan years, representatives of gay organizations entered into a complex set of negotiations over the nature of the confidentiality protections that were to be afforded to AIDS research subjects.
>
> *(Bayer, 1995, para. 12)*

Together, leaders of gay rights organizations and medical researchers established standards for informed consent that effectively changed the role of AIDS patients in the research process from *subjects* to *participants*.

A *participant* is an active and willing member who is voluntarily contributing to the work, while the term *subject* implies passivity—the person on whom research is conducted. As this chapter's first epigraph quotation, from Rebecca Skloot, implies, research involving humans is vastly different from research conducted on more easily observable and controllable subjects such as plants and even mice. The main difference lies in humans' ability and right to choose what they do and what is done to them. Humans must be fully informed about research in which they participate, so they can either consent or not to the study.

Informed Consent

Informed consent is fundamental to conducting research with humans that is legal and ethical. As bioethicist Jessica De Bord (2014) explained, *informed consent* traditionally refers to the process by which a competent adult agrees to, or refuses, a medical procedure, based on thorough understanding of the reasons it is being recommended and its potential benefits and risks. Informed consent originates in the legal and ethical rights of adults to determine what happens to their own bodies (De Bord, 2014). Informed consent laws now extend far beyond medical procedures to all forms of research or intervention involving people. People can benefit from and be harmed by a much broader realm of research than that involving medical procedures. Imagine for a moment a psychological study that could trigger Post-Traumatic Stress Disorder (PTSD) in some subjects/participants. Because myriad forms of research involving human beings have the potential for harm, no matter how seemingly minor, ethics and federal laws require that people participating in surveys, questionnaires, research observations, focus groups, interviews, oral histories, and any other form of research give informed consent to participate.

The Immortal Life of Henrietta Lacks

The 2010 book by Rebecca Skloot, *The Immortal Life of Henrietta Lacks*, was researched for over a decade to bring to light the far-reaching consequences and injustices of unethical research practices. It is about a

> poor black tobacco farmer whose cells—taken without her knowledge in 1951—became one of the most important tools in medicine, vital for developing the polio vaccine, cloning, gene mapping, *in vitro* fertilization, and more. Henrietta's cells have been bought and sold by the billions, yet she remains virtually unknown, and her family can't afford health insurance.

Used across the United States as a freshman convocation and summer reading book, it won many awards including the *Chicago Tribune* Heartland Prize for Non-fiction, the Wellcome Book Prize, the American Association for the Advancement of Science's Prize for Excellence in Science Books, the Audie Award for Best NonFiction Audiobook, and a Medical Journalists' Association Open Book Award. "It's a story inextricably connected to the dark history of experimentation on African Americans, the birth of bioethics, and the legal battles over whether we control the stuff we're made of" (Skloot, 2010). The compelling story of Henrietta Lacks provides undergraduate researchers an example of why human "subjects" need to be informed, consulted with, and treated fairly when involved in research studies. Even if your study does not involve human subjects, the whole topic of ethics in research methods is something with which you, as a researcher, should be familiar. Just about every area of research holds some ethical considerations, even if not as directly as the research conducted on Henrietta Lacks.

Research that appears to have absolutely no risk of harm and/or may even benefit participants is not off the hook from informed consent and ethical review. Informed consent means people are agreeing or declining to participate *with full knowledge*, even when there are no known risks either way. Informed consent also includes people agreeing or declining to participate in research that may benefit themselves or others. Why would anyone decide not to answer a short survey for a professor's research if they did not have to provide their name, could take the survey during class time (so would not have to use free time to do so), and would receive extra credit points for turning it in? The answer is, it doesn't matter. Each of us has the legal right to opt in or out of participating in research without explaining our reasons. Informed consent ensures that people are making the decision with knowledge about what they are agreeing to or declining.

IRB Approval

How do researchers know that they have provided enough information to participants to meet the legal standard of informed consent? How do we guard against unintentionally harmful or ethically questionable research practices? The primary gatekeepers protecting human participants from potential harm or manipulation, and preventing researchers from making ethical or legal violations (even inadvertently), are members of the Institutional Review Board (IRB). Every institution in the US in which research involving humans is conducted—every college and university, research hospital, school district, and any other type of research facility—has, by law, a committee typically known as the IRB. Other countries have similar ethics boards that go by different names, such as Canada's Tri-Council (made up of representatives of three major granting agencies), the United Kingdom's Research Ethics Committee (REC), and the European Union's Ethics Committee. The 1964 "Declaration of Helsinki" by the World Medical Association established international ethical guidelines for research involving human subjects (World Health Organization, 2001).

According to US federal law, an IRB is made up of at least five experts in biomedical and social-behavioral research ethics. Members of the IRB are charged with protecting the rights and welfare of human subjects/participants in research conducted by anyone affiliated with the institution, including faculty, staff, and students of a college or university. The IRB must review and approve all research involving humans before the research may commence. The chairperson of the IRB is responsible for posting readily accessible (usually online) information about ethical and legal requirements for research involving humans, training sessions for researchers, and the IRB review process.

The IRB review process involves the main researcher, known as the *principal investigator* (PI), usually the faculty member overseeing the undergraduate research, and the *co-investigator(s)*, who are the student(s) and anyone else collaborating on the research (e.g., community partners or faculty colleagues of the PI). The PI submits the IRB application and is ultimately responsible for ensuring that the research is carried out in accordance with what is described in the application, after it has been approved. None of the research involving human subjects/participants can begin before IRB approval—not even recruitment of the participants.

In addition to requiring a description of informed consent, IRB applications call for the following explanations:

- how the PI and co-investigators will protect the privacy and confidentiality of all human participants;
- how the participants will be recruited;
- how the participants will be compensated, if applicable;
- where the participants' confidential and/or identifying information will be stored (e.g., on a password-protected hard drive and/or a locking file cabinet)—and who will have access to it;
- how the PI and co-investigators will dispose of confidential and/or identifying information after the study is complete and a certain period of time has passed (e.g., by fully deleting computer files and shredding paper records). Note that IRBs often require the PI to retain records in a secure location for a set period of time, typically three years, after the completion of the study.

If the study includes a survey, a final copy of the survey must be attached. If the study includes interviews, oral histories, and/or focus groups, a list of questions to be asked—often known as the *interview guide* or *protocol*—must be attached. Researchers must stick to the questions on the interview guide, though related follow-up questions are permissible.

The IRB may require revision of the research protocol or even reject the application if required information is missing or incomplete, or if the board determines that the risks of the research are too great. The risks of research are highest when *vulnerable or protected populations* are involved; vulnerable populations include children, people in prison, and people with cognitive impairments, to name a few.

Why Is Training on Human Subjects Research Necessary?

Most US college and university IRBs require everyone conducting research with human subjects/participants to complete human subjects research training every three years. That requirement includes undergraduate researchers. The training is provided by the Collaborative Institutional Training Initiative (CITI), which offers several different online courses and modules. Everyone involved in human subjects research takes the Responsible Conduct of Research CITI course and/or the Human Subjects Research CITI course, which has a Social-Behavioral-Educational track. Additional modules or courses may be required depending on the nature of the research.

Requiring researchers to take online CITI courses and pass the quizzes helps colleges and universities ensure that research conducted in their name and with their support is done so with ethical integrity. Those who have completed CITI training are much more likely to carry out their research legally and ethically. They are informed about appropriate research protocols and the reasons for particular rules.

Completing training in human-subjects research confers benefits on the researchers themselves, beyond the knowledge they gain about ethical research practices. Practically speaking, completing CITI training dramatically decreases the chance that a researcher will submit an IRB application that gets rejected or requires revision. Having to resubmit an IRB application requires extra time and can cause stress for the researchers. It can significantly delay the start of the study, sometimes for weeks, as protocols need to be rewritten and then reviewed again by the IRB. (At a large university, waiting a month or more for a decision from the IRB is not unusual.) Students working within the confines of a semester have no time to waste. Another benefit of completing CITI training is having ethics-course certification among your experiences—a distinctive credential for your résumé and/or graduate-school applications.

How Do I Get Trained?

The IRB chairperson will let the PI know if CITI training is required for the planned research and, if so, which courses need to be taken. Each CITI course takes a few hours but does not need to be completed in one sitting.

If you need to complete CITI training you will not need to pay for the courses. Each college and university has a CITI subscription that covers faculty, staff, and students of the institution.

Before creating an account on the CITI website, find out from the IRB chairperson how your institution handles student registrations and which courses you need to complete. Most likely you will be directed to create an account at www.citiprogram.org/index.cfm?pageID=22 by entering the name of your institution.

After each course module you will be quizzed on its content. The score considered "passing" is set by the IRB. (At our respective universities the passing score is 80%.) Of course, you need a passing score to receive a certification of completion.

Questions for Discussion

- What will happen if I don't take the appropriate steps to protect the rights of participants in my study?
- How do I know what type of training is necessary?
- Will CITI training help me after I graduate?
- How do I choose my participants?

References

Bayer, R. (1995). AIDS, ethics, and activism: Institutional encounters in the epidemic's first decade. In R. E. Bulger, E. M. Bobby and H. V. Fineberg (Eds.), *Society's choices: Social and ethical decision-making in biomedicine*. Washington, DC: National Academies Press. Retrieved from www.ncbi.nlm.nih.gov/books/NBK231965/.

De Bord, J. (2014). Informed consent. In C. H. Braddock and K. A. Edwards (Eds.), *Ethics in medicine*. Seattle, WA: University of Washington School of Medicine. Retrieved from http://depts.washington.edu/bioethx/topics/consent.html.

Hurston, Z. N. (1996). *Dust tracks on a road*. New York: Harper Perennial. Original work published 1942.

Skloot, R. (2010). *The immortal life of Henrietta Lacks*. New York: Broadway Books.

World Health Organization. (2001). Declaration of Helsinki. *Bulletin of the World Health Organization*, *79*(4): 373–374. Retrieved from www.who.int/bulletin/archives/79(4)373.pdf.

5

COLLECTING DATA

> In God we trust. All others must bring data.
>
> W. Edwards Deming

> It is a capital mistake to theorize before one has data.
>
> Sir Arthur Conan Doyle

Summary

This chapter explains the importance of sound research methods. It introduces students to qualitative and quantitative methods and when to use one or the other, as well as when to mix methods. Examples are given of major data-collection strategies for undergraduate research in film, including conducting library research, exploring primary sources, recording one's own observations with research journals and field notes, distributing surveys, and conducting interviews and focus groups. The main differences in methods between arts and humanities scholarship and social science research are described.

Importance of Research Methods

Research is a methodical investigation or inquiry aimed at answering a specific question. The *methodical* approach is what gives a research study rigor and trustworthiness. After learning what is primarily known about the topic area through a review of the literature (see Chapter 2), researchers develop a focused, significant, debatable question (see Chapter 3). As this chapter lays out, researchers then plan their own *methods* for addressing the question. They determine which sources of *data*, or information, would help answer the question and how to access those sources. Purposefully planning methods of data collection and carrying out the research according to that plan (as well as adapting the methods as needed, also based on thoughtful planning) are at the heart of conducting research.

The strength of a research study, therefore, depends most on its *methods*—the processes used to gather data/information to address the research question. Scholars who carefully select the methods best suited to answering the research question set themselves up well for a successful study. A successful study is not necessarily one in which the hypothesis or expected conclusion is proven, but one in which something new and interesting is discovered, and that new and interesting discovery is supported with evidence/data. Sound methods get to that goal.

One of the common missteps we have observed in our mentoring of undergraduate research is a rush to decide on research methods that are obvious and readily accessible. We have had students who tried to rely entirely on secondary sources located through online research, for example, because they were most familiar with that method of information-gathering, even though additional sources of evidence would significantly strengthen their claims. And we have had to guide students away from simply conducting surveys of their peers as their primary research method; although gathering opinions from a group of friends, acquaintances, and/or classmates may be handy, that narrow group of people likely will not provide enough diversity of thought or richness of information to develop a full-fledged conclusion. This chapter is intended to guide student researchers to more thorough, well-planned methods—methods that are well aligned with the research question and goals of the project.

Sound research methods are critical to the success of your entire study because the results completely depend on the quality of the data, and the quality of the data completely depends on the ways they were collected, recorded, and analyzed. Your process of gathering and analyzing the data must be made evident before your results are presented in any dissemination of the research, such as a presentation or research paper. The audience's trust in your findings will either be buttressed or undermined by how well you carried out the study and how well you explained carrying it out.

Establishing Credibility as a Researcher

Well-selected research methods—methods chosen precisely because they get at the particular research question—lead to trustworthy results. In addition to setting up a successful study, sound methods give credibility to you as a researcher. For at least 25 centuries of human thought, the credibility of an author has been a foundation of effective argument, or *rhetoric*. In the 4th century BCE, the classical Greek scientist, philosopher, and teacher Aristotle explained that appealing persuasively to an audience requires *logos, pathos* and *ethos*. Those three parts of a persuasive argument are now known as the *rhetorical triangle*. *Logos* refers literally to the *logic* of one's argument—the reasons, evidence, and explanation that convince others of one's points. *Pathos* concerns appeals to the audience by connecting with them through emotions and values. An example of *pathos* in a research paper about how private soldiers were photographed during the US Civil War is the inclusion of a moving story about a particular private soldier as a means of connecting readers to a historically distant reality (documentary filmmaker Ken Burns uses this stratagem in his *The Civil War* television series for PBS very successfully!). Statistics can be used as a form of *pathos* as well, such as in a report on the number of high-poverty school districts which have had to eliminate their film programs in the past decade, which may stir audience members' sense of justice and appeal to their values of the arts in public education.

Ethos relates to the character of the writer/speaker. The importance of *ethos* to rhetoric/argument derives from the idea that audience members will only be persuaded by the logic of the claims (*logos*) and the appeals to their values (*pathos*) if they trust the person making the argument. That trust is established when those making claims explain with transparency how they arrived at their conclusions—in the case of research, how they gathered their data and why they went about it in the ways they did. If, on the other hand, the audience is not convinced of the credibility and quality of the work of the researcher, they have no reason to accept the claims.

Triangulated, Intentional, and Impartial Data Collection

Triangulation of Data

Establishing your credibility as a researcher and ensuring, as well as possible, the success of your study require collecting data in *triangulated, intentional,* and *impartial* ways. *Triangulated data collection* refers to gathering information in a variety of ways as a system of data "checks and balances." Data from one source can be corroborated or disputed by a different source. When multiple sources of information are brought to bear on a research question, the researcher can attain a more reliable and comprehensive understanding. Consider for example a film research study presented by Hannah Avery, an undergraduate student enrolled in the upper-division seminar *FILM 301: Issues in Lens-Based Media* (MSU-Bozeman, fall 2018), on female and male screenwriters' representation of women characters in contemporary American films and television shows (see Figure 5.1). As Hannah's abstract explains, she decided to frame her study through the lens of multiple theoretical perspectives from feminist and reception film theories to gender and postmodern studies of cinematic representation to better evaluate the writers' choices and viewers' responses. Using solely the feminist theoretical framework, for instance, would have produced a biased study in favor of the perspective of the female writers and spectators. Only by developing a multifaceted methodology through the lens of diverse theoretical perspectives could Hannah arrive at an informed and insightful argument. That work of drawing from multiple theories and data is known as triangulation.

Although the term *triangulation* has led some of our students over the years to conclude that they need exactly three sources of information, the reality is more nuanced than that. The three legs of a simple campstool give it stability; take one away and the stool topples over, but adding legs solidifies it. We prefer to think of triangulation in terms of that metaphorical campstool's overall stability rather than its literal three legs. In other words, triangulated research might require only three sources of information to stand solidly on its claims, but it may need more. Would you accept a comprehensive argument on the way female versus male screenwriters develop women characters just based on the analyses of feminist film theorists? Furthermore, if only depictions of women for the screen by female writers were studied, would you be able to understand the complexity of contemporary television and film female characters? What if, as Hannah decided, male screenwriters were added for consideration? Her research was certainly more thorough and the findings more consequential because of this decision to include male writers. Further triangulation could lead to entirely different types of research findings, such as interviewing (1) film professors that teach screenwriting courses, (2) freshman film students, and (3) senior film students, being sure not to make gender-biased selections.

To plan triangulated research methods, you might brainstorm about the various forms of data that could address your research questions (or parts of a single research question) and organize them into a table something like Table 5.1.

Intentionality in Data Collection

Lest it sound as if more and more sources automatically make research better, we move to the second criterion of sound research methods: intentionality. *Intentional data collection* refers to the careful thinking involved in determining which sources to pursue. What types of data will allow you to gain the information you need?

TABLE 5.1 Triangulated data table

Part 1 of Research Question	First Method of Data Collection for Question 1	Second Method of Data Collection for Question 1	Third Method of Data Collection for Question 1
Part 2 of Research Question	First Method of Data Collection for Question 2	Second Method of Data Collection for Question 2	Third Method of Data Collection for Question 2

By selecting sources of information intentionally and then explaining why you collected data in the ways you did, you avoid a scattershot (random and overly general) approach to research. In Hannah Avery's study of female characters in contemporary American films and television shows, for instance, her intentionality led to choosing a balanced number of women and men screenwriters' work depicting female roles. Simply compiling example after example of contemporary women characters would not have been nearly as effective as using a criterion for selecting female roles written by both women and men writers.

Avoiding Bias and Ensuring Impartiality

The third expectation of credible researchers, *impartiality*, requires effort to reduce potential bias and errors. Biased or otherwise sloppy scholarship undermines the study itself as well as the credibility of the researcher. Bias in research comes in many forms, some of it unconscious on the part of the researcher. It might include preference for or prejudice against a particular outcome that leads to overemphasis on (or ignoring) certain results. If a researcher expects members of a focus group to be enthusiastic about a shared experience, the researcher might glom on to a few stray comments that fit that expectation. On the flip side, if members of the focus group suspect the researcher is hoping for particular responses, they might accommodate that expectation, especially if they have a relationship with the researcher that would benefit

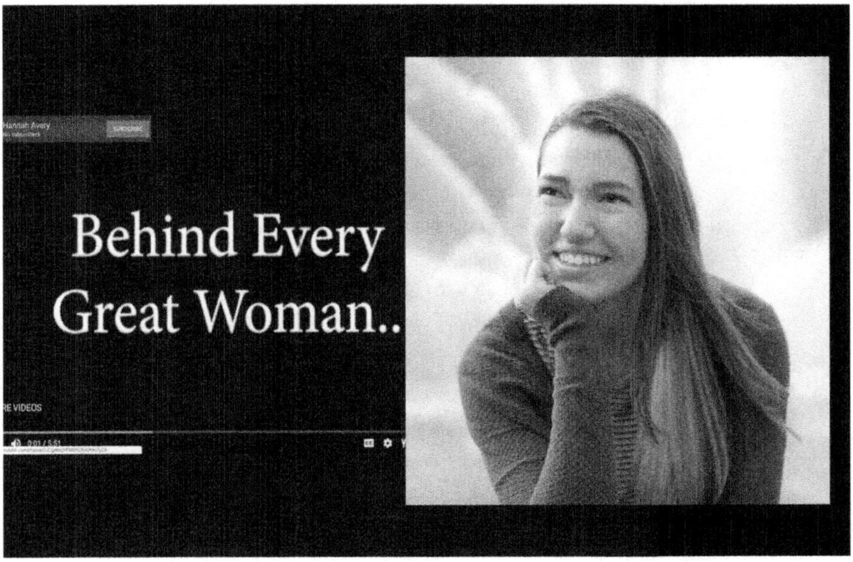

FIGURE 5.1 *Hannah Avery's audiovisual essay "Behind Every Great Woman...," (fall 2018) www.youtube.com/watch?v=sS5AtRRuFNY*

from positive reinforcement. For those very reasons the best practices of focus-group research include having a neutral person facilitate and record the discussion, without the researcher even in the room.

Similarly, the ways in which survey questions are worded may reveal the biases of the researcher and skew responses. Using validated survey instruments designed by researchers with expertise in survey design mitigates those tendencies towards unconscious bias. If you need to develop your own survey, we recommend studying the elements of good design, starting with guidelines for beginning survey researchers, such as Vannette's (2015) "10 Tips for Building Effective Surveys" and asking for feedback on your draft questions from professors who teach research methods.

Even peer-reviewed research articles are likely to reflect the values of the journals that publish them, so overreliance on sources from one journal should be avoided. As these examples indicate, impartial research design requires vigilance. Consistently asking yourself how sources of data could be obtained with the least possibility for bias can lead to helpful ideas for fair and evenhanded methods. Explaining in your method section the steps you took to reduce bias and the chance of errors demonstrates your impartiality and credibility as a researcher. Informed readers can and should be attentive to signs of prejudice and imprecision in reports of research. They will appreciate indications that you collected data carefully and as impartially as possible.

Quantitative, Qualitative, and Mixed Methods Research

How do you decide on the types of research data to triangulate, select intentionally, and collect impartially? One rough breakdown of the types of research data you might gather is *quantitative* and *qualitative*. *Quantitative data* is numerically measurable and reportable information. Quantitative data literally show the calculable quantity or amount of something. Examples include the number or percentage of participants who gave a particular response to a survey question; the average increase in scores between participants' pretest and posttest; the amount of time needed to complete a series of tasks; and even the results of a structural analysis of the use of close-up shots in a film.

Qualitative data cannot be measured numerically; it is descriptive information about the qualities of people's ideas or behaviors, or any other subject of study that requires interpretation rather than calculation. Examples of qualitative data include transcripts of interviews; open-ended written responses on surveys; analysis of the emotions expressed in a film sequence by the protagonist; and evaluations of body language, tone of voice, and/or word choices in a dialogue scene.

Sources of information are rarely exclusively quantitative or qualitative; many can be analyzed in different ways for quantitative or qualitative data, such as pre and posttests that could be evaluated in terms of how many responses were correct (quantitative measure) and/or analyzed for patterns in the open-ended responses (qualitative interpretation). Likewise, researchers often benefit from obtaining both quantitative and qualitative data. Using both types of information to get at different facets of the research question is known as *mixed methods research.*

Quantitative Methods

The following are the most common quantitative methods used by undergraduate researchers in film.

- *Surveys/questionnaires with multiple-choice or Likert-scale responses*: surveys and questionnaires capture demographic and/or opinion data that are self-reported by individuals. A Likert scale is usually made up of five or seven choices aimed at measuring degrees of agreement, from strongly disagree to strongly agree, for example. A Likert scale provides a more nuanced set of responses than simple agree-or-disagree binary choices.
- *Tests of content knowledge, ability, attitude, or skill:* pretest and posttest data are often used to determine whether an intervention, such as a new teaching technique or a particular experience or event, may have affected participants' knowledge or attitudes. The pretest and posttest ask for the same information at different points in time—days, weeks, or months apart.
  Pre and posttests may be given to one group of participants to measure change over time, or distributed to two sets of participants known as the *experimental group* and *control group* in order to make a comparison between them. The experimental group participates in the intervention being studied ("the experiment"), such as a new method of teaching. The control group continues with the status quo. Experimental and control groups usually share basic demographics in common. A study aimed at determining whether *flipped classroom* techniques would improve learning outcomes in a high school Film Studies class could employ flipped classroom techniques with one class (the experimental group) while the other class would learn the content the same way it traditionally has been taught (the control group). In a flipped classroom, content that is usually delivered in lectures in class is now accessed by students outside of class, as homework. In-class time is repurposed for active and experiential learning; students apply the information they read or watched in video-recorded lectures outside of class to collaborative, inquiry-based projects during class.
- *Structural analysis of film or other texts:* a quantitative structural analysis entails some form of counting, such as the number of a type of syntagma in a filmmaker's work (e.g., Christian Metz, 1974) or the words that came up most frequently on an online discussion board.
- *Statistical analysis:* the analysis of statistical data gathered by oneself or previous researchers is a sophisticated quantitative research skill. Statistical

data include a vast array of evidence, from individuals' personal/demographic information to immense sets of organizational and national information.

Qualitative Methods

These are the most common forms of qualitative data in undergraduate research in film.

- *Surveys/questionnaires with open-response questions:* open-response questions invite survey-takers to write out answers to questions that do not lend themselves to either-or or multiple-choice responses. They allow participants to convey a range of ideas, attitudes, and examples, often providing rich information for researchers. (Many surveys of course include both quantitative and qualitative questions.)
- *Interviews:* interviews, which are typically one-on-one interactions in which the participant answers a set of questions posed by the researcher/interviewer, may be audio-recorded with the permission of the participant. Whether the interview is recorded or not, the interviewer usually takes extensive notes during and immediately following the interview.
- *Focus groups:* focus groups are akin to group interviews. A group of people with something in common that is of interest to the researcher (e.g., students in a summer undergraduate research program; attendees of the same film screening; survey respondents who checked the box at the end of the survey indicating their willingness to be contacted for follow-up research) is invited to participate in a discussion about the topic. The group should be small enough that everyone can contribute a response to some or all of the questions—usually between five and 20 participants. The facilitator poses questions to the group and may either encourage a free exchange of responses or suggest a means of equitable participation. Focus groups may be audio-recorded with the informed consent of each participant. Sometimes a notetaker accompanies the facilitator so that the facilitator can attend to the group dynamics without the additional task of writing notes.
- *Document analysis:* some student researchers get the extraordinary opportunity to work with primary sources in an archive or much more accessible online collection. *Primary sources* are original documents or artifacts created in the time period being studied, such as diaries/journals, original film scripts and production notes, letters and other correspondence, and audiovisual recordings. Archives around the world preserve original documents of historical and cultural significance in secure, fireproof cabinets in temperature-controlled, low-humidity rooms, all to ensure that they will not be lost to current and future generations. University library archives, as well as many archives associated with museums, historical societies, and

other public and private libraries, offer rich troves of primary sources for student researchers. You may be required to get a brief training from the archivist and to wear archivist gloves—or you may have to view fragile, high-value pieces through plastic or glass—but those precautions are well worthwhile, as there is nothing quite like the thrill of working with a document written in a world-famous filmmaker's own hand.

- *Digitized library and museum collections:* these have made primary-source research possible from your own computer or your university's library database. Digital photos of documents and film clips bring the archives right to you.
- *Secondary source*: anything that interprets or is otherwise at a remove from a primary text (e.g., an article that includes excerpts of letters) is a secondary source. Your notes in a research journal—capturing key quotations as well as your own film analysis and observations—are invaluable sources of qualitative data. When reading and analyzing a text (whether a film script, a storyboard, production notes or a film clip, to name a few), you could be jotting down ideas that strike you, direct quotations you want to use and cite, questions that pop up in your mind, connections you see to other texts and any number of other thoughts. Those notes, especially if you color-code them according to patterns and/or mark up significant details, are a form of qualitative data analysis.
- *Case study:* empirical observation and analysis of one important case (or a small number of cases) may give deep insight into a broader issue. The "case" may be a person, course, event, or other phenomenon. Lauren Griffith's 2015 National Conference on Undergraduate Research (NCUR) presentation on Hitchcock's use of the same "alluring blonde, with a strong personality" type of female character in his films derived from case studies of three of his movies: *Vertigo* (1958), *Rear Window* (1954), and *North by Northwest* (1959). In analyzing the look and demeanor of the three films' female protagonists, Griffith was able to make a larger assertion about the director's use of an immediately identifiable character type in all of his movies: the *Hitchcock blonde*.
- *Observation* (also called *field observation* or *direct observation*): conducting observations on behaviors or other phenomena in a certain setting can be a valuable qualitative research method when carried out by rigorous researchers who are doing much more than simply watching. Observation research requires detailed field notes about what is observed—a crucial aspect of its methodological rigor. Sometimes the field notes are structured to include certain behaviors or participants while purposely ignoring others in order to focus on a predetermined set of data, such as observation research on cinematographers. Other field notes are open to everything that catches the researcher's attention, without a prediction of what to expect.If the observation is to be conducted covertly (without the

knowledge and consent of those being observed), privacy must be protected, and the IRB will consider whether the research could be conducted effectively with informed participants instead. If the subjects/participants know they are being observed, the researcher must consider the Hawthorne Effect, the psychological phenomenon of people changing their behavior because they are being observed. Such decisions about covert or overt observations are usually discussed in the method section of a research paper.
- *Participant observation:* conducting observations on the behaviors of a group of people while involved with them over a period of time offers a more intimate angle on observation research. Examples of participant observation include student teachers conducting research on student learning in their lead teachers' classrooms; a member of a film crew seeking to determine the most effectual lighting techniques while shooting on location for students interested in documentary filmmaking; and undergraduate researchers in film reflecting on their own and their classmates' experiences in their film studies class as a means of informing future students, as they have done for this book. Like other forms of observation, participant observation requires detailed field notes, though the notes may have to be written immediately after the observation time because participating and note-taking simultaneously may not be possible.

Some forms of research can be quantitative, qualitative, or mixed methods, depending on the types of information to be gathered. Two examples are listed below.

- *Longitudinal study:* empirical observation and analysis of something over a significant period of time (e.g., one-year commitment to editing a film after a particular form of instruction).
- *Pilot study:* collecting data about a new intervention or process while it is carried out for the first time, and analyzing the data to determine the intervention's longer term efficacy.

Note that IRB approval is required for all of these forms of research except when they do not involve people in any way. IRB approval is not required for use of *archival data*—information already collected by other researchers (who had IRB approval) that is now available, with no personally identifiable information, for new researchers to analyze.

Arts and Humanities Methods

You may notice that in some scholarly papers in the arts and humanities, research methods are discussed only briefly or may even be implicit (not explicitly identified). That occurs when the author is using a widely accepted method with which the intended audience would be familiar. An ethnographic study published in a journal dedicated to ethnography, for example, would omit some of the rationale for the selected method. For undergraduate research papers and presentations, however, the method should be made apparent, as the audience is rarely limited to narrow experts.

That being said, you may also notice explanations of scholarly processes that are referred to in other terms. Many scholars in the arts and humanities would not use the word *method* to describe their process of collecting information, as it is traditionally associated with research that is *empirical* (verifiable by observation) or *experimental* (based on scientific tests). Much of the scholarly work conducted in the arts and humanities is *theoretical*, as it builds on existing knowledge to explain or create new concepts/phenomena. Theoretical scholarship is distinct from empirical and experimental research in many ways, as indicated by the different terminology, yet experimental approaches can be applied to creative endeavors as well.

Caleb Chicoine (2018), another undergraduate student enrolled in *FILM 301: Issues in Lens-Based Media* in fall 2018, for example, did a research project that explored the increasingly blurred line between the media of photography and film in the digital age (Figure 5.2). Caleb's work was both theoretical and experimental because: (1) it built on existing theories about the nature of (ontology) and the knowledge functions (epistemology) of film and photography (i.e., Barthes, 1977; Bazin & Gray, 1960; Metz, 1974; Bellour, 2008; Jenkins, 2006; Solomon-Godeau, 1991, 2017, etc.) to understand how digital technology has influenced these systems of theoretical knowledge; and (2) it expanded on existing film and photographic works (i.e., Andy Warhol's films *Sleep*, 1963, *Empire*, 1964 and *Screen tests*, 1964–1966; Jacques Tati's 1967 *Playtime*; Gregory Crewdson's 2019 photographic work, and the like) to generate his lens-based experiment, which is available to view on YouTube.

Scholars doing theoretical and creative work may or may not use the term *method* to describe their process. Alternative terms include *process, technique, approach* (including *theoretical approach* and *critical approach*), *study*, and *analysis*. Caleb, for instance, referred to his experiment as the result of a "scholarly and creative process" because that terminology better fit his work. All of that is to say that various terms may be used in different contexts, but whatever phrasing is used, scholars are expected to describe the methods of their inquiries. In Caleb's case, he explained several parts of his scholarly/creative process in his research project proposal for *FILM 301*:

1. After having become knowledgeable on the current literature related to the fields of photography and film theory, Caleb extrapolated a series of scholarly established criteria used to define the nature and functions of these media. He then performed a structural analysis of photographic and cinematic works that have challenged the boundaries between the media of photography and film to see what criteria are adequate to

understand/define these "hybrid" works. Finally, he applied such criteria to produce his lens-based media experiment (see Figure 5.3).

2. Caleb uploaded his lens-based media experiment on YouTube and distributed questionnaires with multiple-choice responses and surveys with open-response questions among undergraduate students attending MSU-Bozeman, asking them to watch the YouTube link and then fill out the questionnaire and survey questions. He both advertised his experiment using the School of Film & Photography (MSU) Facebook page and, upon his classmates' suggestion, sending the questionnaire and survey questions to the College of Arts & Architecture (CAA) Dean's assistant, so that she could circulate them among the CAA students. The questions were meant to find out whether his lens-based experiment was perceived either as a photographic or film product (or a mix of both).
3. After having gathered the responses, Caleb performed an analysis of the findings, which he presented publicly on December 12, 2018, in the Visual Communications Building at MSU. Due to the limited number of students' responses received, together with the feedback he got during the public presentation of his study, Caleb realized that additional time may be needed to assure adequate completion of his research project. Thus, he will be working on refining his methods and revising his experiment as a part of his BFA (Bachelor of Fine Arts) thesis project.

The above methods align with the student's goals for the project and demonstrate that Caleb possesses the knowledge and ability to do the work.

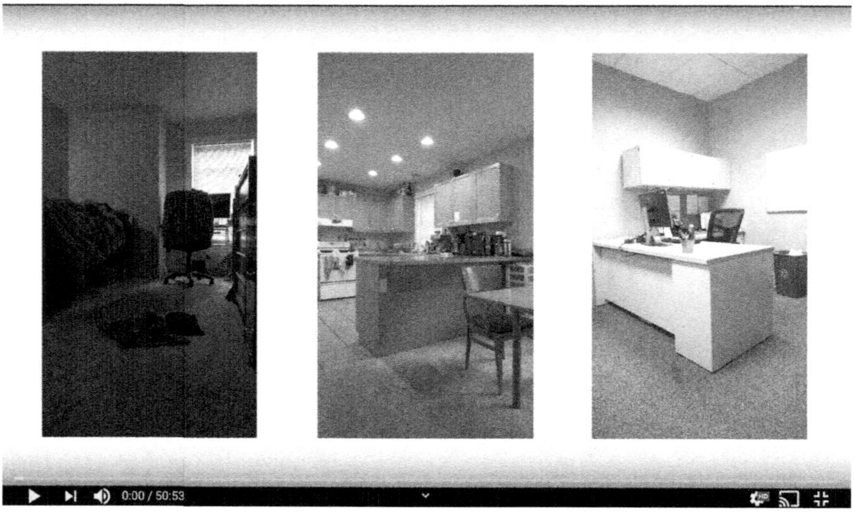

FIGURE 5.2 Caleb Chicoine's lens-based media Experiment (fall 2018) *www.youtube.com/watch?v=ZhRRzNndPSI&feature=youtube.*

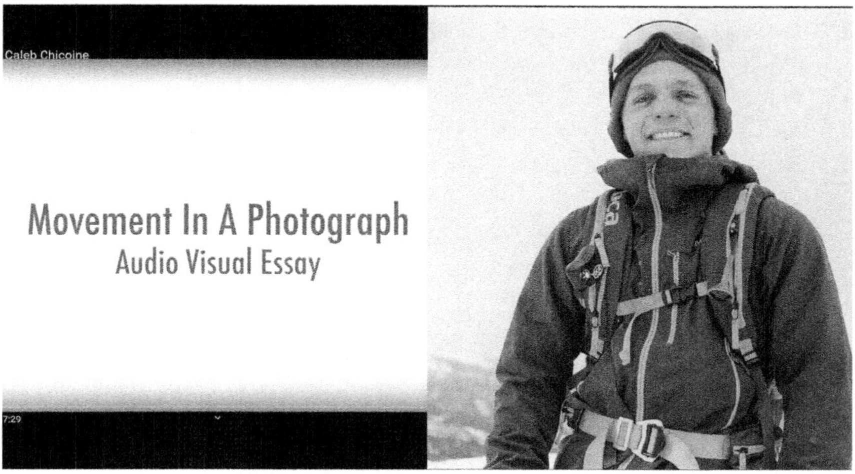

FIGURE 5.3 Caleb Chicoine's Audiovisual essay "Movement in a Photograph" (fall 2018)
www.youtube.com/watch?v=9Jb33Yzuiv8.

Social Science Methods

Some scholarship in the field of film, such as research in film education and film ethnography, would be characterized as social science research, which is mainly *empirical* (verifiable by field and empirical observation), though social scientists also conduct theoretical research. Another way that social scientists conduct theoretical research is in the reverse order: rather than analyzing an existing theory and applying it to their own work, researchers sometimes develop a new theory from their research findings. The term for that form of research is *grounded theory*. The new theory emerges from the "ground" up. A scholar may discover something through empirical research that is not explainable with existing theories. The discovery could be a fluke or a simple anomaly. But if the discovery can be replicated in a different context or otherwise leads to new understanding, the researcher might develop a grounded theory.

Organizing the Method Section of a Research Paper

The scholarly methods or processes are usually explained in a paper after the introduction and the review of the literature. Many professors, journal editors, and other readers of your written work, especially in the social sciences, expect research papers to follow a standard format:

1. *Abstract*, a brief overview (anywhere from 60–250 words, depending on the particular guidelines provided) of the whole paper, with a focus on the methods, results, and implications of the research;

2. *Introduction*, the purposes of which are to orient readers to the topic of inquiry and inspire interest in it;
3. *Literature Review;*
4. *Method;*
5. *Results;*
6. *Discussion;*
7. *Conclusion*, which typically offers next steps and implications of the research.

Academic posters often include each of those sections as well, though the order may be moved around as needed for column space and visual appeal. Oral presentations may also cue the audience when moving to each section, to clarify distinctions between what came from the review of the literature, for example, as opposed to what was learned in the speaker's own research study.

Subsections of the Method Section

Within each of those sections, researchers usually include *subsections* to delineate and organize further the points that go together within each section. Subsections are particularly helpful to aid the reader's understanding of long research papers. We focus here on typical subsections of a method section. The subsections of a Literature Review (see Chapter 2) and Results and Discussion sections (see Chapter 6) are unique to each paper because they emerge from the themes of the particular research study.

The method section of a research paper or poster, however, often includes three standard subsections, organized under their own subheadings:

1. *Participants:* a description of the human subjects/participants involved in the study and how they were recruited or observed, if applicable. In most cases, participants should not be identifiable. Typical information to provide about participants:

   - Number of participants, which may include the number recruited as well as how many actually participated, if applicable;
   - gender breakdown;
   - race and ethnicity breakdown;
   - range of ages and median age;
   - information particular to your participants should be included as well e.g., "All participants were undergraduate students at a large public university in the southeastern United States." This subsection could also describe briefly how participants were recruited (by email, by phone, etc.). A recruitment email, for example, should introduce the

researcher, summarize the purpose of the study, note the university's IRB approval, and request 30 minutes of the participant's time for an interview via phone or over Skype.

2. *Materials:* information about the things used to collect data and/or conduct measurements (e.g., surveys, timed tests, materials the participants read or listened to). This subsection is termed Apparatus when the data were gathered through the use of technical equipment or research instruments (e.g., noise-canceling headphones, eye-movement tracking device, analytical software) or Apparatus and Materials if a mixture of mechanisms were used to collect data. Please note that this subsection may need a different subheading that more accurately captures what kinds of things were used to obtain information (e.g., Survey Instrument may be a better subheading than Materials if the only research material was a survey).
3. *Procedure:* an explanation of how the data were collected, verified, and analyzed. The procedure section usually includes a discussion of *variables*, or factors that can change and therefore could affect the results of the study. Consider, for example, a study of how watching a film trailer on YouTube while studying for Calculus I exams might affect student performance in the exams. There are multiple variables to consider in such a study: how long each participant studied, what times of day/night the studying took place, participants' studying environments and conditions, etc. Rigorous research attempts to control for as many variables as possible, such as by selecting participants with similar study habits and similar grades on previous exams. Any such attempts to limit the number of variables should be noted. Explain the variables that could not be controlled (e.g., participants' studying environments) and acknowledge how they could affect the results. Variables that may weaken the results of the study are a form of *Limitations*. The limitations of your research methods should be acknowledged either as you discuss each method or in summary at the end of the method section.

While the above three subsections are fairly standard, students are often not required to include them in exactly that way, nor to be limited to those three. In a paper on a complex research study, additional subsections are often needed to delineate aspects of the research methods.

Our students often ask us how much detail is needed in the method section. As you can imagine, anyone who has conducted a long, complicated research project could go on and on about each step of the process, but an exhaustive account would not be of interest or need to most audiences. A widely accepted consideration for the degree of detail in a method section is whether future researchers would have enough information to replicate the study in their own settings. One aspect of research is the reliability of results:

the extent to which the results would be consistent if the study were carried out again with similar conditions. Reliability can only be tested if each researcher's methods are spelled out with enough clarity for others to run the investigation again. We recommend trying to strike a balance between presenting clear, replicable information about stages of your research process and not going into excruciating detail. Reading method sections of published papers in your topic area is the best way of understanding where that balance lies.

More about Acknowledging the Limitations of the Research

Every research study has certain limitations: it is limited by the number of survey respondents, or the amount of time over which a change is studied or the inherent bias of the researcher, just to name a few examples. Some limitations are unavoidable and expected. When the limitations will undermine the results of your research, however, you need to use an alternative method of data collection. If a student conducting interviews for her/his project were to receive informed consent from only a small percentage of interviewees, she/he would need to adjust her/his methods or add another form of data collection for triangulation. When the limitations are avoidable (such as when your presence in a focus group could prompt less-than-honest responses, and someone else could facilitate the focus group instead), you are expected to do your best to prevent them.

Unavoidable limitations that you anticipate ahead of time should be noted in the method section. What are the limitations in each form of data you are collecting? For example, were you only able to study one group of people (an experimental group) without a control group for comparison? Was the single semester you had for your film studies project an insufficient amount of time to measure significant differences in pre- and posttests? There is no need to document each and every imperfection in your research process; only the factors that likely weakened the project in noticeable ways need to be acknowledged. Later, when you discuss the results (see Chapter 6), you can speculate on how some results may have been affected by the limitations.

Other Means of Organizing Research Methods

Earlier in this chapter we noted that various disciplines use different terms for *methods*, as well as different ways of organizing scholarly writing. Those differences are not arbitrary or accidental, of course. Each academic discipline is distinguished by its *epistemology*, or its theories and ways of knowing. Epistemology encompasses why and how people in a particular field of study gain knowledge: how we know what we know, which methods are used to teach and discover knowledge, which forms of evidence are considered valid, where knowledge originates, and where its limits might be. It stands to reason that scholars operating under different epistemologies would pursue new knowledge in divergent ways and therefore write and speak about their processes in divergent ways.

A good example of the different terminology reflecting different epistemologies is the word *Procedure*, which is particularly suited to empirical and experimental research. Scholars making empirical observations or running experiments must take great care with their research protocol or procedure. To guard against bias in their observations, to measure accurately, to make equal comparisons, and for many other reasons, empirical and experimental researchers need to follow established procedures. They know that their results will only be meaningful if their data are collected and recorded in precise, methodical steps. Detailing their procedure in the method section of a research paper is understandably expected.

The procedures followed by theoretical and creative scholars are not usually so rigorous or clear-cut—nor do they need to be. A great deal of the scholarly work done in the arts and humanities is interpretive. There is no single, established procedure for analyzing a film, much less for producing one! Individual scholars take their own approaches to theoretical and creative projects, and those approaches are not necessarily linear or prescriptive. Creative projects in the arts, as well as in many other fields, are notoriously ill-structured. We know a scholar of "pure mathematics" who studies concepts so abstract they have no real-world referents; when asked to describe her methods of constructing proofs she said simply, "I think about the problem for a really long time." Imagine explaining the Procedure for that research method!

Students conducting scholarly work that does not fit the methods and terminology of empirical or experimental research have an array of options for describing their processes, including the following two, which could also serve as subheadings:

- *Research Design*: a summary of the investigation (the research question/goal and a few objectives of the study) and the major stages of gathering information to address the question/goal. The stages of information-gathering may be organized *chronologically* (starting with the first step and concluding with the last) or *thematically* (clustering related steps together).
- *Theoretical Approach* (also called *Critical Approach* or *Methodological Approach*): an explanation of the theory (or theories) that was foundational to the research and how that existing theory was applied to your own study. We recommend starting by summarizing the theory and then demonstrating its relevance to your research question. A theoretical idea may be used as a kind of lens for examining primary or secondary sources or other qualitative data; it may offer a methodological approach that you can adapt for your own investigation; and/or a theory may be brought into dialogue with other theories to create a richer understanding of the topic of study.

Questions for Discussion

- Are there standard ways to collect data?
- Which data collection methods are appropriate for my topic (qualitative and/or quantitative methods)?
- How do I judge whether my sample size is appropriate?

References

Barthes, R. (1977). Rhetoric of the image. In S. Heath (Ed. and trans.), *Image, music, text* (pp. 32–51). New York: Hill and Wang.

Bazin, A., & Gray, H. (1960). The ontology of the photographic image. *Film Quarterly, 13*(4): 4–9.

Bellour, R. (2008). Concerning the photographic. In J. A. Suárez, K. Beckman and J. Ma (Eds.), *Still moving: Between cinema and photography* (pp. 253–276). Durham, NC: Duke University Press.

Chicoine, C. (2018, October 8). *Lens-based experiment for FILM 301: Issues in lens-based media* [Video file]. Retrieved from www.youtube.com/watch?v=ZhRRzNndPSI&feature=youtube.

Crewdson, G. (2019). *The broad*. Retrieved from www.thebroad.org/art/gregory-crewdson.

Deming, E. (n.d.). Data analytics. *Tibco blog*. Retrieved from www.tibco.com/blog/2013/06/28/19781/.

Doyle, A. C. (1892). *The adventures of Sherlock Holmes*. London: George Newnes, Ltd.

Jenkins, H. (2006). *Convergence culture: Where old and new media collide*. New York: New York University Press.

Metz, C. (1974). *Film language: A semiotics of the cinema*. Chicago, IL: The University of Chicago Press.

Solomon-Godeau, A. (1991). *Photography at the dock. Essays on photographic history, institution, and practices*. Minneapolis, MN: University of Minnesota Press.

Solomon-Godeau, A. (2017). *Photography after photography: Gender, genre, history*. Durham, NC: Duke University Press.

Tati, J. (Director). (1967). *Playtime*. [Motion picture].

Vannette, D. (2015). 10 tips for building effective surveys. *Qualtrics*. Retrieved from www.qualtrics.com/blog/10-tips-for-building-effective-surveys/.

Warhol, A. (Producer and Director). (1963). *Sleep*. [Motion picture].

Warhol, A. (Producer and Director). (1964). *Empire*. [Motion picture].

Warhol, A. (Producer and Director). (1964–1966). *Screen tests*. [Motion pictures].

6

ANALYZING AND SYNTHESIZING DATA

> Analysis and synthesis are different mental muscles to serve different purposes.
>
> Pearl Zhu

> Analysis is the art of creation through destruction.
>
> P. S. Baber

Summary

The results or findings are the most substantive part of conducting research. This chapter outlines how research results and interpretation of those results are reported in different disciplines and types of papers and presentations. It provides prompts for freewriting or otherwise thinking about the implications of data. While a full exploration of qualitative and quantitative data analysis is beyond the scope of this text, this chapter includes fundamental information about the terms and techniques involved in analyzing different types of information. It discusses the importance of writing an annotated bibliography, triangulating results, identifying overarching themes, and aligning the discussion of research results with the research questions and the review of the literature. The chapter concludes with a reminder about acknowledging any limitations of the research that significantly affect the results.

Results and Discussion

The *results* (or *findings*) of your study constitute what you have learned from the research process. The results include the data along with your analysis or interpretation of the data. Merely reporting the data is not enough. The point of research is the *analysis* and *interpretation* of what the data signify.

In most reports of scholarly work the results/findings are explained right after the methods/process. In APA-style social science papers, the *results* are reported separately from the *discussion*. The results section gives a basic explanation of the data, and the subsequent discussion section provides more thorough interpretation of the results and explains the wider implications of what was discovered. In papers and presentations in the arts and humanities, however, the results or findings are usually interpreted while they are reported. There is no divide between the results and discussion—or between the results and the researcher's interpretation and statement of implications.

Analyzing Research Data

Knowing the etymology (origin) of the verb *analyze* can be a useful means of understanding what is really called for when you are asked to analyze information. The Latin origin of *analysis* translates to the "resolution of anything complex into simple elements" (analysis, 2010). In that original concept of analysis as the breaking down of complex ideas, analysis is posited as the opposite of *synthesis*, which refers to putting parts back into a coherent whole. That idea effectively informs the task of data analysis, which is very much about breaking apart complex information into simpler parts. The Greek etymology of *analysis* adds another facet to this understanding: "a breaking up, a loosening, releasing"; the verb form in Greek is "to set free; to loose a ship from its moorings" (analysis, 2010). Imagine, for a moment, what that version of analysis might look like in undergraduate research. What would it mean to "loosen" or "release" research data? How does the image of a ship set free of its moorings represent something about the task of analyzing information? We see the work of data analysis as analogous to the Latin and Greek origins of the English word. Analysis is an act of setting free into the world the knowledge contained in quantitative and qualitative data. The analyzer's work of breaking the data apart helps others make sense of the information. The researcher's analysis could even be described as loosening up the densely packed evidence, allowing others to see and understand the component parts.

Analysis is what gives meaning to the quantitative and qualitative data you have collected. The data do not hold meaning in and of themselves; it is your analytical work that translates for others what the information actually signifies. This chapter offers tools and techniques for doing that important work of making meaning from data.

Data Analysis Exercise

Examine each piece of data and freewrite answers to the following questions:

- What is interesting/exciting/notable about this piece of information?
- What is the story it can tell?
- Do you think this data point misrepresents what is really going on?
- What, if anything, is disappointing about it?
- Is it consistent with anything you found in your review of the literature? Does it contradict anything you read in the research literature?
- How could it be most effectively presented? In narrative form? In tables or graphs? Key quotations? (Quotations may come from textual analysis, from research participants, from your own research journal, etc.)

Identifying Themes in the Data

The analysis of data is about figuring out the *implications* (or conclusions that can be drawn) of what was discovered. To help our students start to organize their research results we ask them to list and then freewrite about the three to five themes they have learned from their research (the implications). The next step is to compose a topic sentence for each of those themes: a specific, clear, supportable claim about what the data indicate.

We recommend going from there (composing topic sentences on a few clear themes) to organizing data around each of those topic sentences—perhaps by creating an outline or flow chart. Structure the outline by those topic sentences rather than by each piece of data. This is important: the data do not organize themselves. You, as the researcher, are the agent. You decide the ordering of points, and you plug in the data as evidence for those points. We have seen it go the wrong way too many times: the surveys say *a*, the primary sources say *b* and *c*, and many of the secondary sources seem to corroborate the survey respondents (*a*), but a few others say something entirely different (*d* and *e*). When research reports are organized by the data they are messy and confusing, whipping around from one piece of evidence to the next without a sense of control or clear meaning. Successful researchers analyze the data first to identify the implications/themes. The implications of the research are the most interesting points. Then researchers figure out which pieces of data support each of those implications. The difference is enormous between listing a bunch of data that needs to be made sense of and stating clear, focused claims backed up by data.

The data may be represented as evidence in many different forms, including textual evidence (quotations and paraphrases); quotations from survey responses, interviews, or focus groups; and/or tables or graphs of quantitative data. However the data are represented, remember that they play a supporting role. They are the backup to the claims you make.

Analyzing Quantitative Data

A full explanation of how to analyze quantitative data is beyond the scope of this book. Students who have taken a course in quantitative research methods may be able to conduct a *multivariate analysis* of their data, which involves the examination of multiple variables in the data in relationship to one another (e.g., correlations among 300 college-student participants' ages, genders, years of playing an instrument, and number of minutes spent practicing per week). However, that level of analysis requires statistical calculation skills that are not typically expected in the fields of film studies and film production. This discussion sticks to the terms and types of calculations involved in *univariate* (single variable) and *bivariate* (two variables in interaction with each other) quantitative analysis.

If your research involves a quantitative survey, questionnaire, and/or tests, you have an array of software platforms for building the research instrument, distributing it, collecting data, and even doing preliminary analysis. Platforms such as Survey Monkey, Wufoo, and Qualtrics generate reports and allow users to download data into Excel to create customized spreadsheets and conduct analysis. While those user-friendly ways of reporting data help even those without statistical training to capture and compare data, the researcher's own analysis is needed to explain the relationships within and significance of the information. The following explanations are intended to guide that analysis with regard to fundamental quantitative data. The terms used here apply to most types of quantitative data, including those discussed in Chapter 5: surveys/questionnaires, pre- and posttests, structural analysis, and statistical analysis.

Correlation

Correlation is the relationship between two or more data points, such that when one piece of data changes for a certain sample of the population, the other changes too—either in the same or opposite direction. For example, there is a statistical correlation, or relationship, between the highest level of education a group of people have completed and their income levels. There is also a correlation/relationship (though in the opposite direction) between a population's highest level of education completed and their rates of cigarette smoking. Correlation is not the same as *causation*. Correlation indicates that a relationship exists but does not on its own show that one thing caused the other.

Direct Correlation/Positive Correlation/Direct Relationship

These three interchangeable terms all refer to a "positive" relationship between two or more data points. A positive relationship means that when one data point increases, the other does too; when one decreases, so does the other. For example, a population's highest level of education completed and their income levels have a positive correlation or direct relationship, according to many studies. When one is high, the other tends to be too; when one is low, the other usually is as well.

Inverse Correlation/Negative Correlation/Inverse Relationship

These interchangeable terms all indicate an inverse or negative correlation between two or more data points; the data points go in opposite directions when there is a negative correlation. When one increases, the other tends to decrease, and vice versa. Using the same example set above, one would see in many studies that highest education completed tends to have an inverse relationship with rates of cigarette smoking. In other words, the more education a person completes, the less likely that person is to smoke cigarettes on a regular basis. The negative correlation occurs the opposite way too: someone who smokes cigarettes frequently is less likely to have completed college.

Frequency Distribution

A frequency distribution is a display of how often (how frequently) members of a particular population sample gave particular responses (or did particular behaviors or said particular words). A frequency distribution table shows how many participants gave each response (on a survey or test question) or how many times a phenomenon occurred (in a structural analysis).

For the purposes of defining some key terms, consider a survey of 92 film students that includes the question: *How many years have you been using Adobe Premiere as editing software?* The multiple-choice options are (a) less than 1 semester; (b) 1–2 semesters; (c) 3–4 semesters; (d) 4 semesters or more; and e) I don't use Adobe Premiere. Table 6.1 outlines the responses based on gender identity.

Table 6.2 shows the *frequency distribution* by gender of the particular response (d) *4 semesters or more.* The frequency distribution of male students who reported using Adobe Premiere as editing software for 4 semesters or more is 28. These data could be used for a bivariate analysis of gender identity correlated with years of using Adobe Premiere.

Basic Statistical Terms

- *Mean:* average of all the scores (using the mean has drawbacks when there are extreme or outlier scores, which skew the mean).
- *Median:* the middle score when all responses are ranked.
- *Mode:* the most frequently occurring score or phenomenon.
- *Range:* the difference between the highest and lowest responses.
- *Standard deviation:* How much participants' scores differ from the mean (average) score (i.e., the deviation of each score from the mean/average).

TABLE 6.1 Length of time using Adobe Premiere (AP) as editing software, by gender identity

Gender	*< 1 semester*	*1–2 semesters*	*3–4 semesters*	*> 4 semesters*	*I don't use AP*	*Total*
Female	0	16	4	0	12	32
Male	0	4	16	28	8	56
Other or Prefer Not to Answer	0	4	0	0	0	4
Total	0	24	20	28	20	92

TABLE 6.2 4 semesters or more of using Adobe Premiere as editing software, by gender identity

Gender identity	*Frequency*	*Percent (%)*
Female	0	0
Male	28	100
Other or Prefer Not to Answer	0	0
Total	28	100

Structural Analysis in Film

An example of structural analysis in film is provided by undergraduate student Hannah Avery's study of female characters in contemporary American films and television shows (see Chapter 5). In order to assess whether strong and round women characters are mainly conceived by female or male screenwriters, she created a survey that asked participants to first watch two predecided television shows, *Buffy the Vampire Slayer* (television series 1996–2003) and *Gilmore Girls* (television series 2000–2007), and then answers the survey's multiple-choice questions about whom they thought was the "strongest" and most realistic female lead: was it Buffy Summers (conceived by male writer Joss Whedon) or Lorelai Gilmore (created by female writer Amy Sherman-Palladino)? The participants' answers were displayed in a table so that the reader could easily see the biggest disparities. Hannah then compared the participants' responses with subjective annotations about what personality traits a "strong and believable" female character should possess (her notes were taken while reading current scholarly literature on the subject). The quantitative data (participants' responses) were not meaningful on their own. It was the student's analysis of what it means to be a "strong and relatable female character" that illuminated the information and allowed Hannah to put forth an interesting set of conclusions about the decisions of female versus male writers with regard to creating television roles for women.

Analyzing Qualitative Data

The metaphor of unpacking luggage is an apt description of how to analyze qualitative data, including primary and secondary source texts, research journal notes, participant responses (from open-response survey questions, interviews, or focus groups), and any other information that cannot be quantified. Imagine taking each piece of qualitative data, one by one, out of its place and holding it up for examination. What is interesting about it? How is it different from the other things (the other data points) right next to it? With what else does it logically go? Asking and answering those kinds of questions about qualitative data help bring the information to life, in a way. Thinking about the interesting qualities of each piece of data helps you to put together a meaningful story from your own interpretation of the data.

Coding

An example of qualitative data analysis comes from a student who conducted interviews with undergraduate film majors about movie celebrities who have been accused of sexual misconduct after the "Harvey Weinstein scandal." The student researcher asked open-ended questions about the perceived "sincerity" of the accused stars' public apologies, then she recorded the responses and transcribed them. The student's transcription of the responses was only the first step of data analysis. Next, she examined the transcript for patterns. Every time the idea of "authentic" or "sincere" came up in the participants' responses, she highlighted the text in yellow. When participants described the celebrities' apologies as being "bogus," the comments were highlighted in blue. Indications of no longer wanting to watch any television shows and films produced, written, directed, or starred in or by the accused celebrities were highlighted in green. Then, examining a multicolored transcript of the interview responses, the student researcher could identify some prominent themes—namely that the film student participants mentioned "bogus" more frequently than "authentic" or "sincere," and that most of them would stop watching films and television shows featuring the accused celebrities.

That form of qualitative data analysis is known as *coding*. Similar data—or pieces of data that share the same idea—are coded by theme. The coding can be done by hand on hard copies using colored highlighters or annotations by pen or pencil (e.g., asterisk as one code, check mark as another, etc.) or on a computer using the highlighter function in word-processing programs. For large data sets, coding can be done using analytical software (e.g., SPSS, NVivo, Dedoose) that organizes pieces of text by code/theme.

Limitations of the Research

As explained in Chapter 5, every research study has certain limitations. Every researcher is limited by time, resources, access to information, etc. When the limitations of the study significantly affect results, researchers need to identify the issue and explain the ramifications. What if, for example, a student studying a lesser-known but important filmmaker discovered in the course of the research that primary sources and other archival materials about the filmmaker were less informative than the student first thought they would be? Not all would be lost, especially if the filmmaker's movies were available for analysis; but the influences from the filmmaker's personal relationships, thought to factor into her work, could not be fairly determined from the few journal entries and letters that survive. That lack of information and its impact on the research should be noted and discussed.

Questions for Discussion

- Are you most drawn to qualitative or quantitative analysis?
- What about mixed methods research?
- What happens when the results are not what you expected?

References

Analysis. (2010). *Online etymology dictionary*. Retrieved from www.etymonline.com/index.php?allowed_in_frame=0&search=analysis.

Baber, P. S. (2010). *Cassie draws the universe* (Google books version). New York: iUniverse.

Zhu, P. (2016). *Thinkingaire: 100 game-changing digital mindsets to compete for the future* (Kindle edition). Pennsauken, NJ: BookBaby.

7

CITING SOURCES

> People seldom improve when they have no model but themselves to copy after.
>
> Oliver Goldsmith

> I get a lot of big ideas, and occasionally I actually come up with one myself.
>
> M. C. Humphreys

Summary

Responsible scholars give credit to other researchers and authors by correctly acknowledging ideas that are not their own. Giving credit is accomplished through the use of citations and bibliographies. This chapter discusses MLA and APA guidelines as well as some of the reasons for using different citation and reference styles. Plagiarism encompasses a wide spectrum of behaviors, from outright word-for-word copying of another's work to artful paraphrasing that restates another author's idea without acknowledgment. We provide guidelines and resources to help students navigate the challenge of properly citing others' ideas and avoiding unethical uses of information.

Rationale

Research is the pursuit of knowledge and truth, so conducting research honestly is fundamental to the task. Every scholar has the responsibility to demonstrate absolute integrity in the reporting of data, in acknowledging the sources of ideas and information, and in providing thorough and correct documentation of those sources.

In this chapter we seek to shift some common perspectives on research integrity and the citation and documentation of sources. Many of our students have expressed a sense of fear or frustration about the topic of citations and bibliographies. They have too often been made to feel as if they could fail an assignment due to plagiarism for making an honest and fairly minor mistake in citation. On the other end of the spectrum we have had many students who assume that in a world of easy access to free information, there is no big deal in sharing and appropriating each other's work. Both attitudes are missing the mark and creating unnecessary problems for students, especially those involved in undergraduate research. Let us see if we can redefine the mark by clarifying a reasonable goal of honesty and integrity in scholarly work.

Plagiarism

The definition of plagiarism is taking someone else's ideas and representing them as your own. Plagiarism is a form of theft, as the ideas and hard work of one person are taken without their consent by someone else who hopes to benefit from them. In the US, and many other countries, we share a legal standard and cultural understanding that each person's ideas (which are usually represented in the products of the ideas, such as works of art and pieces of writing) are uniquely their own. When the ideas are shared publicly—whether in the form of a film, blog post, song, essay, etc.—the creator/writer enters into an implicit trust with those who encounter them. The original creator/writer trusts that shared values and legal standards will keep their own name attached to it—that anyone else who shares or builds upon their work will give them the credit that is due.

Students and other scholars who incorporate others' ideas into their own are required to identify clearly the original sources of the ideas, no matter how easily accessible the information may be. Even those not intending to steal or cause harm may be committing ethics violations that have consequences, so it is incumbent on researchers to document the sources of information. When they intend to give credit but make an omission or other mistake students may be more guilty of sloppy scholarship than outright plagiarism. While it may not be an illegal offense, sloppy scholarship should be guarded against by taking care in the work and double-checking that all sources of information are correctly credited.

The intentional appropriation of others' ideas without giving credit is much more serious, of course. University policies and academic publishers dictate serious consequences for those who are caught plagiarizing or committing other violations in research ethics. Strict policies and severe consequences are intended to discourage such violations, for if plagiarism occurs without significant repercussions everyone's work is diminished. For that reason, plagiarism can ruin a scholar's career. Other ethical and legal violations include fabricating or falsifying data and improperly treating human subjects/participants (including any violation of IRB (Institutional Review Board) guidelines).

Why There Are Different Citation and Documentation Styles

In our various academic disciplines, we are all in agreement about the utmost importance of academic integrity and the lawful and ethical crediting of the sources of ideas. We have different guidelines for exactly how we do that crediting, though, based in our disciplinary epistemologies, or theories and ways of knowing (see Chapter 5). When students are required to use Modern Language Association (MLA) format in their first-year writing course and, just when they have that down, are expected to switch to the American Psychological Association (APA) style in their education or other social science classes, and then Chicago style in communication studies, they may be understandably frustrated. We have heard more than once students bemoaning different citation styles as a conspiracy to drive them mad.

Believe it or not, however, there are some sound reasons for the different expectations. We have found that understanding the epistemologies and underlying reasons for different citation and bibliographic styles helps ease the frustration. Graff and Birkenstein's (2014) *"They Say, I Say": The Moves that Matter in Academic Writing* very helpfully addresses the concept of templates in academic writing. Graff and Birkenstein point out that many of our disciplinary conventions follow certain patterns or templates, and that by learning some of the main ones we can master aspects of academic writing with more enthusiasm.

Our friend and colleague Herb Childress applies the idea of templates to understanding different citation systems and the disciplinary values they represent. Dr. Childress uses examples of MLA and APA parenthetical citations and bibliographic entries to make the point. MLA parenthetical citations require the author's last name and the page number on which the idea is stated. In APA format the parenthetical citation includes the author's last name and year of publication. The only time the page number is provided is when the text is quoted directly, which is rare in APA papers. Why the differences? MLA is the format used in the humanities, disciplines in which elegant writing and textual analysis are highly valued. Humanities scholars need the page number of an idea because reading the actual text, whether directly quoted or not, is important to them. APA, however, is used most often in social sciences, where different primary values are in play: timeliness—hence the use of the year of publication in the parenthetical citation—and the empirical/experimental findings themselves, as opposed to the prose in which they were reported. That is why APA papers include few, if any, direct quotations: the findings are what matter, not the way in which the researchers expressed them, so paraphrases do not lose the essence of the ideas.

The bibliographic entries of each style likewise reflect disciplinary priorities. On an MLA Works Cited page, authors' first and last names are listed, whereas APA uses last name only and initials. Why? The fullness of the human person is not only a subject of study but a deeply held value in the humanities. A scholar's full name conveys more about that person than his or her initials, including in many cases his or her gender identity. The scientific approach favored in disciplines that use APA style has a preference for more neutrality. There is no way to know the gender identity of a scholar from first and middle initials alone, and that is considered a good thing in objective research. Another notable difference between the two bibliographic styles is the placement of the year of publication: near the end of the entry in MLA Works Cited, but right after the authors' names—second thing in the entry—in APA References. The privileging of timely research is again the reason for the early placement of the date in APA References entries. In the humanities, however, timeliness may not matter at all. For people who study ancient and classical texts, there is timelessness in human wisdom. The year of publication is one of the least important pieces of information, so it is relegated to the end of the entry.

The OWL at Purdue

Even though we can understand some of the reasons for different citation and bibliographic styles, it is difficult to master and remember them. And even when we do master one or two styles with which we work most regularly, a new edition of the style book is published, and we have some new details to try to keep in mind. Fortunately, holding all of that in one's own mind is not necessary beyond the basics, and keeping up with the changes can now be automatic. Thanks to the Online Writing Lab (OWL) at Purdue University, examples of citations and bibliographic entries for a wide variety of sources in several styles are readily and immediately available. We recommend bookmarking the website (https://owl.english.purdue.edu/owl/) and keeping it open while writing. Through a quick search and a look at some examples, anyone can be sure of correct, up-to-date citing and referencing.

Questions for Discussion

- What "counts" as plagiarism?
- What if you didn't mean to plagiarize?
- What are the consequences for plagiarism in undergraduate research?
- How can I identify typical mistakes in citing sources?

References

Goldsmith, O. (n.d.). Retrieved from www.goodreads.com/author/show/65124. Oliver_Goldsmith.

Graff, G., & Birkenstein, C. (2014). *"They say, I say": The moves that matter in academic writing*. New York: W. W. Norton.

Humphreys, M. C. (2011). *Some inspiration for the overenthusiastic* (Kindle edition). Original publication in 1983.

8

DISSEMINATION OF RESULTS

Cinema should make you forget you are sitting in a theater.

Roman Polanski

I want to make movies that pierce people's hearts and touch them in some way, even if it's just for the night while they're in the cinema; in that moment, I want to bring actual tears to their eyes and goosebumps to their skin.

Russell Crowe

The cinema is really built for the big screen and big sound, so that a person can go into another world and have an experience.

David Lynch

The TV scientist who mutters sadly, "The experiment is a failure; we have failed to achieve what we had hoped for," is suffering mainly from a bad script writer. An experiment is never a failure solely because it fails to achieve predicted results. An experiment is a failure only when it also fails to adequately test the hypothesis in question, when the data it produces don't prove anything one way or another.

Robert M. Pirsig

Summary

Included in the CUR (Council on Undergraduate Research) definition of undergraduate research is the phrase "contribution to the discipline." Like faculty scholarship, undergraduate research contributes to the discipline through dissemination of the work to other scholars, in the form of publications, conference presentations, performances, and exhibits. There is a growing number of opportunities for students to present, publish, and show their work, and this chapter provides a guide for film students and faculty alike as to the various venues, conferences, symposia, film events, and journals available to students.

Why Share Your Work?

The key attribute that transforms ordinary students doing research assignments into *scholars* is the dissemination of research results. Scholars are part of a *scholarly community* that learns from each other and advances the field of study. That learning from each other can only occur, of course, when scholars share their findings. One purpose of conducting research is to inform one's own thinking. But the more important reason to do research is to contribute to the discovery and creation of new knowledge. In sharing new knowledge researchers further not only their own but also many others' understanding about the topic of study and contribute to the progression of the field.

Dissemination as a Defining Feature of Undergraduate Research

The definition of "undergraduate research" according to the national organization CUR is "a faculty-mentored inquiry or investigation conducted by a student that *makes an original intellectual or creative contribution to the discipline*" (Council on Undergraduate Research, 2019; emphasis added). The mentored inquiry or investigation would be incomplete without the *contribution* (through dissemination) to the discipline, or to another community as appropriate. That "original … contribution to the discipline" is a very high standard; any scholar's work could shoot for that goal and not always get there, for any number of reasons. It could turn out that another scholar made the discovery first. Sometimes limitations of studies (see Chapter 5) are more significant than initially realized and then undermine the results. Or, even after a thoughtfully chosen design, a study may not go as planned, and the data could be inconclusive. Achieving publishable results that make a notable disciplinary contribution is not the only standard for successful undergraduate research, nor is it the only reason to disseminate findings. We usually talk with our students in terms of a slightly edited version of the CUR definition of undergraduate research: a faculty-mentored investigation that *seeks to make* an original intellectual or creative contribution. *Seeking to make* a contribution puts the focus on the process and purpose of conducting scholarly work. It does not depend on an entirely successful contribution. Having an orientation for your research efforts towards a community of disciplinary experts, peers, and/or practitioners (e.g., filmmakers, teachers, and therapists) makes your work more meaningful and scholarly than if you were gathering information solely for your own knowledge base.

We have found it even more useful to identify what makes undergraduate research a "high-impact practice" (Kuh, 2008)—the characteristics or criteria of impactful scholarly experiences, rather than a one-size-fits-all definition. Osborn and Karukstis (2009) laid out four criteria of high-quality undergraduate research: mentorship by faculty, original work, acceptability in the discipline, and dissemination. In this chapter we are most interested in that last criterion, dissemination. Dissemination is considered a defining characteristic of undergraduate research because sharing the results of scholarly work with an audience of academics, peers, experts in the field, a community of practice (a group of people who share a common interest and wish to learn from each other about it), and/or the general public completes the research process and is a powerful learning experience in its own right.

Engaging with an Authentic Audience

Have you ever wondered about the point of writing a research paper that only your instructor would ever read—and perhaps only cursorily, along with dozens of other students' assignments? We remember feeling let down at times during our student years, after investing late-night hours and some pretty good ideas in writing an essay, only to send it into the apparent void of a professor's paper pile. Our best professors wrote thoughtful responses to each student's work, and a couple of them even talked with us about it, but those were few and far between.

On the other hand, when students have the chance to engage with an authentic audience for their work beyond a single instructor, they say they devote more time and effort to it. As university faculty we have witnessed the difference in the quality of student work when it is to be disseminated in some way. The research and writing simply matter more when other people will read and respond to the product. As social creatures, perhaps all of us are hard-wired to want to connect with others through our ideas and efforts. When others find our work thought-provoking, when they ask questions about it, and/or when they offer productive feedback, we tend to want to meet their expectations for good-quality work. For all of these reasons—the contributions that can be made to a scholarly community and field of study, the logical completion of the research process, and the higher level of effort and engagement inspired by addressing an audience—sharing the work is an essential aspect of undergraduate research.

What You Will Gain from Presenting and Publishing Your Scholarly Work

You may have heard the worrisome news reported by the National Center for Education Statistics (NCES) (2018) that the unemployment rate for recent college graduates in the US remains higher than it was before the 2008 recession. And while student-loan debt is at its highest point in history, wages for young adults have remained flat since 2000 (NCES, 2018). The Federal Reserve Bank (2019) has concluded that underemployment—which is defined as part-time employment for those who want to work full-time and/or employment in low-skilled jobs for people with college degrees—for recent college graduates is even higher: over 40% in the US.

The problem of the persistently high unemployment and underemployment rates for recent college graduates appears to be based, at least in part, in employers' beliefs that millennials are unprepared for skilled work. A major survey of business and nonprofit leaders commissioned by the Association of American Colleges & Universities (AAC&U) found that employers see recent college graduates as ill-prepared for career success (Hart Research Associates, 2015). Employers gave low grades to recent college graduates on all of AAC&U's learning outcomes of a college education, including six skills deemed most important for career success across a range of nonprofit and for-profit industries: (1) oral communication, (2) working effectively on teams, (3) written communication, (4) ethical decision-making, (5) critical thinking and analysis, and (6) applying knowledge to real-world problems.

Oral Communication Skills

Implications of the research are that students who develop particularly valued skills are likely to stand out in a very tough employment environment. Nearly all business and nonprofit leaders surveyed said those six skills are more important than a job candidate's major or the university they attended (Hart Research Associates, 2015). In other words, students should be focused more on oral and written communication and critical, real-world problem-solving skills than worrying about the most marketable majors or the prominence of their university. All of the skills most valued by employers are developed exceptionally well through undergraduate research. And the top-ranked skill, oral communication, is principally cultivated through presenting scholarly work. Speaking articulately and confidently and engaging interpersonally with a diversity of people are oral communication skills that need extensive practice to develop.

It would not be at all surprising if you were reluctant (or even deathly afraid) to develop oral communication skills by giving research presentations. Just about everyone experiences nervousness about public speaking, and for many the very idea brings on acute anxiety. According to the Chapman University (2018) Survey of American Fears, glossophobia—also known as stage fright or fear of public speaking—is one of the most common forms of personal anxiety. Fortunately, there is a plethora of online and print resources to help manage anxiety about public speaking. More severe phobia can be eased through therapy, relaxation techniques, or hypnosis.

The best strategy of all for overcoming a fear of presenting is to practice over and over again, preferably in low-stakes settings. Take opportunities to present in less stressful situations, such as in a class with people you know and can trust to be on your side, or in a student research symposium on your campus, where dozens or even hundreds of your peers are going through the same experience along with you. Public speaking is truly something that gets easier by doing it. We recommend starting out with poster presentations, if feasible. Our students have found it much less nerve-racking to speak for a few minutes with one or two audience members at a time than to give a more formal talk. After even one poster presentation you will likely gain confidence in your ability to present your work and may feel more ready to try an oral presentation in a friendly environment. (Preparing poster and oral presentations is addressed later in this chapter.)

Written Communication Skills

The other critical career skill that is enhanced by sharing your research is written communication. Writing the content of an oral or poster presentation is an excellent means of developing drafting and revision skills. Writing about the results of research is especially suited to common workplace writing situations, such as reports and presentation materials. Showing a willingness to revise written work has been cited by employers as a rare and valuable trait. Your work to revise presentations—especially in consolidating a large amount of information into a succinct and effective poster or talk—can be noted in cover letters and interviews to your benefit.

Publishing your undergraduate research will take that distinction in written communication skills to a whole new level. Composing a substantial paper that will be carefully read by an audience—as opposed to the quick grasp they would get from presentation slides or a poster—requires writing acumen and a longer process of drafting and revision. The work likely will pay off exceedingly well, though. Student papers published in Bridgewater State University's journal of undergraduate research, *The Undergraduate Review*, have been downloaded well *over a million times*. Students whose work appears in the journal, which is published in print as well as electronic form, report being asked about their research papers during interviews for internships, jobs, and graduate and professional school. They can include a link to their published paper in electronic applications, offering an at-the-ready writing sample that is not only well written, but also copy-edited and nicely laid out by the journal editors. Since the published papers show up in online searches too, the students have discovered that when their names are Googled by potential employers or graduate admissions officers, what shows up, at or near the top of the results, is their published research. The benefits of that exposure of a student's best work are incalculable.

Where Can You Share Your Work?

The Rhetorical Situation

As you may have learned in an English Composition course, the *audience, context*, and *purpose* of a piece of writing constitute its *rhetorical situation*, or the circumstances in which an argument is made. Like the concept of the rhetorical triangle explained in Chapter 5, the theory of the *rhetorical situation* derives from Aristotle's *Rhetoric*, an ancient Greek philosophical text about the art of effective speaking and writing. Bitzer (1968) adapted the concept for modern presenters and writers to explain how their claims are shaped by the intended audience (including readers), the context (or setting or framework in which the presenter/writer is working), and its purpose. The following examples of each aspect of the rhetorical situation—audience, context, and purpose—are intended to help illustrate its function. Imagine sharing your research in a venue mainly attended by your college or university's film professors. As experts in the field of study, the *audience* of film professors would expect high-level scholarly work. You might, for example, decide to include theoretical ideas with which only people who study film theory would be familiar. Alternatively, what if you were to present that same work in a talk at a multidisciplinary undergraduate conference attended by hundreds of college students majoring in a broad range of fields, many of whom have never taken a film course? In that presentation you would either omit some of the theory or include only a few key points with clear explanations. The audience determines a great deal of which content you share and how you present it.

The *context* (circumstance, setting, or framework) is the second determining factor. The presentation to the film faculty could occur in a departmental thesis defense, where you are expected to give a formal talk followed by challenging questions from the faculty. Your skill in answering the questions as well as your ability to present your most important results succinctly and clearly are being evaluated for a grade, and may even determine whether you graduate with honors. That high-stakes context would undoubtedly influence your selection of information and how you prepare for the questions. If, however, instead of justifying your work at a thesis defense you were presenting in a less intense situation, both the substance and style of your presentation would be different. Consider, for example, presenting a poster at your university's annual undergraduate research symposium that is held on campus. Members of that same departmental film faculty might stop by your poster. Yet you would interact with them less formally, one or two at a time, rather than addressing the whole department at once. What you say to them would probably vary, based on how well you know each professor and how acquainted each is with your work. The context shapes the content, format, and design of the presentation.

The *purpose* of sharing the work also affects its substance and form. If you received an undergraduate research grant from the department to support your work you would likely need to report to faculty on the selection committee about what you accomplished at the end of the grant period. Such a report could include major findings, challenges you encountered and how you addressed them, and a statement of gratitude for the opportunities afforded by the funding. But what if the grant were renewable and you wanted to request additional funds? You would still show what you accomplished with the first grant, but you would need to add a convincing explanation of how much further you would like to take the project and how a second round of funding would make that possible. In that grant-renewal request you would have a distinctly different purpose (asking for more money) and therefore would need to alter your report to achieve the hoped-for outcome. Each purpose has its own demands, and meeting those particular demands is essential to success.

This section is titled "Where can you share your work?" The answer to that question is contingent on the rhetorical situation, or the network of audience, context, and purpose. The main options are to publish your research in an academic journal, to present it at a conference, or to show it at a film screening event, and there are multiple outlets and venues within those broad categories. The following possibilities for dissemination of undergraduate research in film begin with the most accessible opportunities and move roughly to the most selective.

Campus Symposium of Undergraduate Research

As the benefits of undergraduate research as a high-impact practice become ever more widely recognized, most four-year colleges and universities in the US now offer opportunities for students to share their scholarly work in a campus symposium or showcase of undergraduate research, most often held at the end of the academic year. Some of those events feature poster presentations exclusively, while others include a mix of poster and oral presentations and, in some cases, film screenings, art displays, dance and theatre performances. The size and atmosphere of campus symposia vary a great deal too. On some campuses, student-presenters are selected through a review process, whereas at other institutions everyone who wants to present is welcome, and many faculty members even make a symposium presentation a course requirement, especially for capstones and other research-intensive courses. Awards for the highest quality research projects are given at many campus symposia.

Presenting in a campus symposium or showcase is an outstanding opportunity for several reasons. The symposium audience—other students, faculty and administrators, and some presenters' family members—offers a valuable and gratifying experience in addressing a real-world audience. Over the years we have each witnessed hundreds of students heading to their campus-symposium presentations with apprehension or dread, only to hear them say immediately afterward and, often, in the months and years that follow, that it was not nearly as intimidating as they had feared. Many of our students have even reported that the experience was fun. One of the most satisfying professional experiences for each of us is that first conversation with a student after a presentation. Students express relief that they overcame nervousness to give a solid presentation and, most exciting, gratitude for the experience of talking with people interested in their work. It has been through positive experiences at campus symposia that most of our students who have gone on to present at national conferences gained the confidence to do so.

We encourage you to present your work in whatever venue is available on your campus, whether a showcase of work from your department or school, or a university-wide event. The practice is invaluable, and each presentation is a legitimate point of distinction on your résumé, especially with oral communication skills so highly valued. If your college or university does not yet hold a symposium of student scholarship, you have a few options to pursue. The first is, with the support of faculty who know the quality of your work, you and some peers could request an opportunity in the department to share your work in panel presentations or posters. Many universities' larger events started with individual department efforts. And plenty of individual departments find that they value the small seminar-style symposia so much that they will keep hosting those events even if a larger showcase takes off on their campus. The second option is to locate an institution nearby that hosts an annual symposium of student work and ask whether students from neighboring campuses could participate. Our campus symposia welcome student-presenters from community colleges in the area. Finally, you may find a state or regional undergraduate research conference with the welcoming environment of a campus-based event. The large Commonwealth of Massachusetts annual conference hosted by UMass-Amherst, for example, has a high rate of acceptance and an inclusive feel.

National, State, and Regional Undergraduate Research Conferences

Statewide and regional conferences of undergraduate research offer a moderate "step-up" in presentation experience. Many such meetings accept most applicants, as they are not intended to be highly selective, but to give as many students as possible the opportunity to share their work beyond their home campuses.

The more selective state conferences are "posters at the capitol" events, for which a set number of students across that state are chosen to present posters, usually in the capitol building itself. The purposes of such events, beyond the great experience and prestige afforded the student-presenters, are to show legislators and their staff members the importance and quality of research taking place in their districts and across the state and, more or less directly, advocate for research and higher-education funding in the state. Traditionally, most of the posters at the capitol feature science, technology, engineering, and mathematics (STEM) research, but the rising recognition of the importance of scholarly work and funding for STEAM—STEM plus the arts—has brought more presentations from film and other arts disciplines.

As faculty and administrators with longtime participation in the National Conference on Undergraduate Research (NCUR) we cannot say enough about what a valuable experience that annual event offers for student-presenters. NCUR has an over-30-year tradition of bringing together thousands of students from across the nation—as well as dozens from other countries—each year on a different college campus to present their research and creative scholarship. Over 3,500 students presented at Kennesaw State University in Georgia in April 2019, in the form of posters, oral presentations, art exhibits with gallery talks, and lecture-recitals (in which students in the performing arts perform a piece of music or dance and provide a brief lecture on it). NCUR has a high rate of acceptances, usually over 80%, and maintains strong quality in its presentations. Besides the distinction of presenting at a national conference with a large, engaged audience, NCUR offers the opportunity to meet students in your own field and every major imaginable from across the country and the world. The conference hosts a graduate-school fair of hundreds of different programs, inspiring keynote speakers, and social events. Inexpensive excursions in the local area are often also available on the Saturday the conference ends.

Disciplinary Academic Meetings/Conferences

As the tide of undergraduate research has swept through higher education in the last two decades, many of the disciplinary professional organizations in which university faculty participate and present their scholarly work have provided venues for undergraduates in their respective areas to present too. Our universities' undergraduate research offices regularly receive notifications of new opportunities for students to present at academic organizations' regional and national meetings. Most of those organizations have carved out a session for undergraduates within the larger meeting, giving students the dual benefit of attending presentations by scholars in their field of study while having a space for presenting at an undergraduate level. Putting undergraduates side by side with renowned scholars can be intimidating for the students. Nonetheless, a few disciplinary conferences have gone that route, successfully bringing together undergraduates, graduate students, and professors in shared sessions.

Opportunities in film include the Society for Cinema and Media Studies Undergraduate Hub (2019), an organization that "seeks to further media study within higher education and the wider cultural sphere, and to serve as a resource for scholars, teachers, administrators, and the public" (para. 3), including by organizing the SCMS-U undergraduate annual conferences. Previously known as the Midwest Undergraduate Film and Television Conference, SCMS-U undergraduate conferences are held annually across various North American and Canadian universities, enthusiastically supporting undergraduate research in cinema history and theory and media studies.

Undergraduate Research Journals

Undergraduate students who get their work published are most often published in a journal of student work. Many colleges and universities publish their own students' scholarship in a campus-based journal, in electronic and/or print format. In addition to campus-based journals, a few college and university consortia (associations of several institutions joined by region or mission), such as the Council of Public Liberal Arts Colleges, and state-university systems publish journals featuring work by students at any of the member institutions.

A few student journals publish work by undergraduates in multiple disciplines from any college or university. They include *Focus*, a nationally recognized undergraduate film journal focusing on critical studies in media culture (www.filmandmedia.ucsb.edu/academics/focus-media-journal/), *American Journal of Undergraduate Research* (www.ajuronline.org/), *Journal of Undergraduate Research and Scholarly Excellence* (http://jur.colostate.edu/), *The Honors Review*, which welcomes undergraduate students' papers on any topic (https://honorsreview.wordpress.com/), and *The Stanford Undergraduate Research Journal*, which welcomes submissions in all disciplines (https://surj.stanford.edu/).

Peer-Reviewed Academic Journals

If your audience is made up of professionals in the field and your purpose is to demonstrate high-level competence as a scholar, perhaps with the goal of attending a selective graduate program in an area of film, publishing your work in a peer-reviewed journal may be your goal (see Chapter 2 for an explanation of the peer-review process). In that case, your research would have to be not just mentored by a professor but actually be a professional collaboration between your faculty mentor and yourself. Publishing in a peer-reviewed journal is the "gold standard," or most prestigious level, of dissemination of scholarly work. Undergraduate research is not usually considered for such publications unless the work is co-authored with a faculty member, as meeting the standards for such journals usually requires expertise in the field that most scholars attain through graduate study and in their academic careers. If you are collaborating with a professor on a shared project, your professor may already be thinking in terms of a peer-reviewed publication. Having papers accepted for such journals is an expectation for university faculty as they seek tenure and promotion; in addition, most academics enjoy disseminating their work as part of their engagement in the field of study. If a peer-reviewed journal publication is the goal, your professor will likely take the lead as first author, but the expectations for your contributions will likely be demanding. Experts in the field of study are the arbiters of the quality of the research and writing.

Forms of Dissemination

Abstract

In order to present your scholarly work, you will first need to submit an *abstract*, or summary, of the work. The abstract is the basis for conference organizers vetting your application to present (sometimes, though rarely, additional documents such as a personal statement are requested). If you are accepted to present, your abstract will appear in the conference program.

An abstract is a one-paragraph overview of a project or study. An abstract for a conference may need to be as brief as 60 words or may go as long as 350 words (for NCUR); check the conference's Call for Abstracts for requirements. Write the abstract after your work is complete, or is at least far enough along that you have initial findings to report. The abstract focuses on results and the significance of the work. It is written in past tense for most disciplines, but can be in the present tense for film projects. The abstract for a conference presentation should not be written in future tense. (In other words, you should not submit the same abstract if you created one before you began your work, for a research proposal.)

At the top of the page include a thoughtful, interesting, and informative title, with the first letter of each main word capitalized—no quotation marks, italics, or underlining. Be sure to include the name(s) of the author(s). An abstract is usually structured with the following parts:

- *Sentences 1–2: INTRODUCTION/CONTEXT* (or more on a longer abstract: Context/Background/Need). What is the problem, question, need, or important context that prompted your work?
- *Sentences 2–3: THESIS STATEMENT.* The purpose/focus of the study or project. You can state the purpose explicitly e.g., "The purpose of this research was to determine … to examine … to analyze … to learn … to investigate … to assess … to research … to create … to compose …"
- *The next 2–3 sentences: METHODOLOGY.* Statement of the methods or process you undertook in order to fulfill the purpose.
- *The rest of the abstract (2–5 sentences): RESULTS OF STUDY.* Explanation of the results of your work (what you discovered or created) and its significance/implications. Consider how your project relates to others' published work. How will other scholars or the discipline overall benefit from

your results? If applicable, how could you or other scholars take your study further?

Posters

Academic posters constitute a distinct genre that calls for planning and presentation of ideas in ways very different from research essays. A poster should not be designed as a shortened research paper with images added. Like any other text—in any genre or rhetorical situation—posters should be designed with the audience, context, and purpose in mind.

Poster presentations offer certain advantages over traditional modes of presenting scholarship. For one, many more presenters and audience members can be accommodated during a single session, as opposed to the panels of just three or four presenters at a time that are typical in oral-presentation sessions or film screening panels. So as participation in undergraduate research grows at most institutions, accommodating hundreds of presenters at campus symposia and other conferences will be more feasible with at least some of the arts and humanities students (not just those in the sciences) presenting posters. Another asset of poster presenting is that students are required to think about their work in new ways, including how to articulate it more succinctly and in a different format. Poster presenters not only gain skills in consolidating points into the content of the poster, but also in their "poster talk" or "elevator speech"—the two–three-minute synopsis of the study they need to have ready to deliver. Preparing posters also helps students develop skills of visual rhetoric and design thinking, as they consider how to represent their points in visually appealing configurations.

The rhetorical situation (audience, context, and purpose) of poster presentations prompts additional considerations. Because of the opportunities for rich one-on-one interactions with audience members, poster presenters should ensure that the research question, purpose of the study, and major findings are immediately clear. If audience members can grasp the main points right away, the interactions can lead to more nuanced discussion. Consider what an engaged audience member needs to understand quickly in order to ask informed questions during the session. At the same time, think about what a casual observer should walk away with after a briefer perusal of the poster. The uniqueness or distinctiveness of the work should be evident.

Research posters usually include the following parts:

- Summary/Abstract: 2–3-sentence thesis;
- brief introductory/contextual information, including the research question(s);
- theory or critical approach of the researcher;
- explanation of the process or methods;
- findings/results/main argument;

- significance of the work;
- key quotations from primary texts, participants, and/or the research paper, if applicable;
- photos, maps, illustrations, graphs, etc. should make up at least one-third of the poster;
- bibliography, if brief (long bibliographies can be made available as handouts and/or as shared cloud documents).

The poster document is usually created as a single PowerPoint slide, set up with the dimensions of the poster. A typical size is 42 inches in width by 36–38 inches in height, though some conferences have smaller boards available and will therefore require smaller posters. The following suggestions are for the structure and design of the poster:

- At the top, include the title, presenter's name, mentor's name, and your university's and/or sponsoring organization's name and logo.
- Below that heading of the title and names, set up three or four equal-sized columns for text and images.
- The text for most of the poster should be in 32–70-point type so that it is readable at a distance of a few feet. The title can be larger (80–100-point), and captions for images can be smaller (22–24-point).
- Use a white or light background; it makes the poster easier to read. Keeping a white background also costs less to print because less ink is used.
- Use dark, coordinating colors for the body of the text, headings, borders, and lines, etc.
- Align the columns and use text boxes and borders to create neat lines and a sense of order. Avoid "jagged edges" by placing borders around some text boxes and fully justifying text, i.e., aligning it with both margins.
- Follow a logical sequence and structure for reading left to right and top to bottom.
- Maintain consistency in fonts, styles, sizes of text, and width of text boxes.
- Keep some "white space" for ease of reading and visual calm.
- Break up large amounts of text with images that you have permission to use and that are cited. Text should take up less than two-thirds of the poster.
- Make sure that photos and logos are of high resolution. They should not appear pixilated when viewing the poster at 100% zoom.
- Proofread meticulously before sending the document to the printer and, if possible, ask at least one other person to proofread it too. Minor errors are easy to miss on a computer screen but show up large on a poster.

In addition to the above guidelines, we recommend "Poster-making 101" by Professor Brian Pfohl at Bates College, available online at http://abacus.bates.edu/~bpfohl/posters/#essentials.

Oral Presentations

Oral presentations include several of the elements of posters. See the bullet points under "Research posters usually include the following parts". The images and bibliography can be presented on slides, which accompany most oral presentations. Although the basic elements of research presentations are present, no matter the format, differences in genre between posters and talks require distinct considerations. An oral presentation requires a more formal, planned out, scripted (to some extent) presentation *in the moment*. The content of a poster is mostly fixed, so the live presenting is short and less formal—a few minutes at most with each member of the audience. Oral presenters, however, have a longer time with the audience (usually 12–15 minutes, plus a few minutes for answering audience questions) that is fixed and often strictly enforced; staying focused and organized is essential to completing the presentation in the scheduled session.

Presenters of talks cultivate highly valued skills of public speaking that include effective use of body language, eye contact, and voice projection in addition to the writing and rhetorical skills developed by working on the content. Our best advice for preparing oral presentations is first to think about the engaging presentations you have attended, as well as those that were unsuccessful in maintaining your interest. What have other presenters done to maintain your attention or to turn you off from their presentation? How have you seen slides and other visual aids used effectively and ineffectively during oral presentations? We find with our students that it is easy to identify what has gone poorly in ineffective presentations—everything from the speaker reading straight from notes without making adequate eye contact with the audience, to reading straight from the slides, back facing the audience; from low voice volume to verbal tics and other nervous habits; from misspellings and typos on slides to mispronunciation of important terms. Simply avoiding those goes a long way towards giving a good oral presentation.

As you prepare your script and slides, consider what a nonexpert could reasonably retain without losing interest, while also ensuring that you engage knowledgeable audience members. That balance usually requires briefly defining some key terms and theories before moving straight to the results and significance of your work.

In addition to writing the script and designing slides, oral presenters should prepare for audience questions. Work with your faculty mentor and classmates to brainstorm what kinds of questions you should anticipate and how you will answer them. It is just as helpful to prepare what to say when you do not know the answer to an audience question. There is no shame in acknowledging the limits of your study or explaining that the scope of your work did not encompass what is being asked. If you are prepared for responding you will be far less anxious about difficult questions.

Audiovisual Essays

Audiovisual essays are a unique form of presenting scholarship in film. They include the components and format of both an oral presentation and a written essay, with an audiovisual portion added. An audiovisual essay about the greatest villain that director Quentin Tarantino conceived for the screen, Colonel Landa in *Inglourious Basterds* (2009), by a film undergraduate student attending the School of Film and Photography at MSU stood out as an exemplar. The audiovisual essay began with a montage sequence of the unforgettable cast of villains populating Tarantino's film universe, juxtaposing a poignant selection of clips featuring their evil behaviors. The student's visual juxtapositions are accompanied by his witty voice-over commentary, which not only keeps the audience engaged, but also helps him to get his point across in a much more forceful and convincing manner than an oral presentation would. By using film language to build arguments about films, undergraduate students become more aware of cinema's rhetorical and ideological power, using it to their own advantage. Audiovisual essays are becoming increasingly popular as a form of presentation at film conferences around the world (see Chapter 12 for further information about the audiovisual format).

Journal Articles

In order to prepare a manuscript of your undergraduate research for possible publication, we recommend the following considerations.

The first step is to determine early on that publication is your goal so that you orient yourself from the beginning to do work that could be publishable. Writing a publishable paper starts well in advance of the actual writing. Thinking about whether you want to publish your work at the beginning of your research, when you are focusing the topic and research question, is not too soon. That early goal can help you set up a study that takes on something new, interesting, timely, and significant enough to interest journal editors, reviewers, and readers.

You would also need to decide early on what type of paper to write. Full articles of 15–30 pages are the most rigorous and thorough academic papers. They are completed reports of scholarship of importance in the field. Research briefs are much shorter pieces (typically two–eight pages) that summarize the research and highlight the most important findings and implications. Practice-based papers of varying length include scholarly research but focus on community-based or other practitioner work, with implications for people doing work in schools, therapeutic settings, and other places in the community.

Various journals publish certain types of papers and often have particular page-length requirements. Choosing the target journal—the right journal for your work—is therefore important in the early stages as well. It can be difficult to select the right journal unless you are aiming for a campus undergraduate research journal, so plan to spend some time researching the best option to submit to first. Do not submit your work to more than one journal at the same time. A way to determine whether a journal is the right one for your work is to look at the articles it has recently published. Is yours at a similar level of work and within the scope of what the journal publishes?

Keep in mind the criteria that the reviewers will be using to evaluate your paper. The journal guidelines may include evaluation criteria. If not, questions such as these are fairly typical for academic journals:

- Does the paper contain new and interesting material?
- Are points presented concisely and in a well-organized format?
- Are the methods explained in a way that they can be replicated?
- Are the findings/results presented clearly and convincingly?
- Is the analysis/discussion relevant and insightful?
- Are the implications/conclusions supported by the evidence presented?
- Are the vocabulary, style, and tone at a high level of sophistication?
- Are any figures, tables, and images necessary and well designed?
- Are all sources cited in the text and included in the bibliography?

Pay close attention to the journal's submission guidelines. They generally include detailed expectations for the format of papers, submission procedures, and copyright policies. Most journal editors will not waste time on manuscripts that do not align with the guidelines.

Questions for Discussion

- What are you most apprehensive about prior to presenting?
- How can you put your best foot forward?
- How can you exhibit your work for maximum impact?
- What do you feel you will gain from the experience?

References

Aristotle. (2018). *Rhetoric* (C. D. C. Reeve, trans.). Indianapolis, IN: Hackett Publishing. Original work published 4th century BCE.

Bitzer, L. F. (1968). The rhetorical situation. *Philosophy and Rhetoric, 1*(1): 1–14.

Chapman University. (2018). America's top fears. Retrieved from https://blogs.chapman.edu/wilkinson/2018/10/16/americas-top-fears-2018/.

Council on Undergraduate Research. (2019). Mission. Retrieved from www.cur.org/who/organization/mission/.

Federal Reserve Bank. (2019). Underemployment. The labor market for recent college graduates. Retrieved from www.newyorkfed.org/research/college-labor-market/college-labor-market_underemployment_rates.html.

Hart Research Associates. (2015). *Falling short? College learning and career success*. Retrieved from www.aacu.org/sites/default/files/files/LEAP/2015employerstudentsurvey.pdf.

Kuh, G. D. (2008). *High-impact educational practices: What they are, who has access to them, and why they matter.* Washington, DC: Association of American Colleges and Universities.

National Center for Education Statistics. (2018). Employment rates of college graduates. Retrieved from https://nces.ed.gov/fastfacts/display.asp?id=561.

Osborn, J., & Karukstis, K. (2009). The benefits of undergraduate research, scholarship, and creative activity. In M. K. Boyd and J. L. Wesemann (Eds.), *Broadening participation in undergraduate research: Fostering excellence and enhancing the impact* (pp. 41–53). Washington, DC: Council on Undergraduate Research.

Pirsig, R. M. (1974). *Zen and the art of motorcycle maintenance: An inquiry into values.* New York: William Morrow and Co.

Society for Cinema and Media Studies (SCMS) Undergraduate Hub. (2019). Retrieved from www.cmstudies.org/page/about_us.

9

THE PROCESS OF MAKING A FILM AS RESEARCH

> In order to write scripts, you must first study the great novels and dramas of the world. You must consider why they are great. Where does the emotion come from that you feel as you read them? What degree of passion did the author have to have, what level of meticulousness did he have to command, in order to portray the characters and events as he did? You must read thoroughly, to the point where you can grasp all these things. You must also see the great films. You must read the great screenplays and study the film theories of the great directors. If your goal is to become a film director, you must master screenwriting.
>
> Akira Kurosawa

> A film is a petrified fountain of thought.
>
> Jean Cocteau

Summary

This chapter will discuss how the preproduction, production, and postproduction stages of the filmmaking process can be considered as original contributions within the discipline of film, and therefore as valuable as peer-reviewed publications in other disciplines. In this discussion, particular attention is paid to the writing of film students' artistic statements as a way to reflect upon their creative and technical decisions during the filmmaking process. It is by becoming aware of their creative vision and stylistic choices that film students can rightfully make the case that they are artists, not just craftsmen learning a trade. Overall, the purpose of this chapter is to investigate the criteria for assessing the strength of a film project, what kind of background research needs to be performed, and how to document such a process. A variety of filmmaking artistic statements in the realm of film are included to act as a springboard for critical and creative inquiry by undergraduate film majors.

Introduction

Undergraduate students' research training in film varies greatly, from college freshmen choosing an idea for a short film or a topic for a 1,500 word film essay, to senior students planning the production of a feature length film or the writing of a 3,000 word research paper, and depending on whether the film program emphasizes technical skills or a humanities-based course of study. Whether the process of research is meant to support the completion of a film essay or the production of a movie, how is it usually performed? What kind of academic rigor does it entail? How has the advent of digital technology impacted the ways in which research in film is conducted and disseminated? This chapter will explore the criteria for evaluating the strength of projects in film production, what background research needs to be undertaken and documented, and how such work might be received by a variety of audiences from film critics and academic scholars to the average movie enthusiast.

What Is the Process?

In the digital age, it has become easier than ever to produce a film. Not only can undergraduate students shoot at different frame rates, record narration, add background music and sound effects, and edit a film using an iPhone, they can also browse through a wide range of professional filmmaking tutorials online (e.g., LinkedIn Learning, nofilmschool.com, and the like) to find creative solutions to potential technical obstacles. Yet, this cannot be classified as rigorous academic research. Undergraduate research projects in film require both a solid technical foundation in film production (e.g., scriptwriting, storyboarding, production design, cinematography, sound recording, and editing) and advanced critical thinking and research skills. Developing such skills takes time, commitment, and the consistent support of dedicated faculty mentors.

First and foremost, in order to develop the research skills necessary to produce a compelling film, undergraduate students must be motivated, committed, persistent, passionate, and willing to practice those skills on a regular basis. Learning the art of filmmaking from the preproduction to the postproduction stages entails consistent practice of cinematic techniques as well as the critical analysis of a wide range of filmmaking styles. Extensive background training in scriptwriting, storyboarding, production design skills, cinematography, acting, directing, and editing in conjunction with film studies knowledge, will then allow the undergraduate film student to draw upon the skills needed to produce innovative and meaningful work.

The research process is a vital part in writing innovative and thought-provoking film scripts. While developing an idea for a script, undergraduate film students need to become a mini authority on the subject they decide to tackle. By reading renowned movie scripts that deal with similar topics, by researching scholarly articles on related film subjects, and by studying the stylistic approaches of selected filmmakers, undergraduate students learn to recognize formal conventions used in effective scriptwriting and moviemaking. Performing textual analyses of screenplays, films, and articles is a time-intensive process that can yield results similar to executing a scientific study. Like the scientist's task of sketching out a general hypothesis before delving into the details at the microlevel, planning a film involves thinking about the big picture first and later paying more attention to specific components. In fact, when preparing a movie story, film students need to first jot down the main idea for a script (c. 50 words), then write a treatment (a 10-20 page document that tells the whole story focusing on a few key turning points in the plot), and only later fill in the details for the final script (a script for a feature film is usually 110–120 pages).

Inspiration for a film topic can come from a wide variety of sources and stimuli, including knowledge of film history and theory, exposure to different types of filmmaking styles, personal experience, and a keen interest in understanding human behavior. As mentioned before, undergraduate students are required to spend a large amount of time reviewing film scripts, watching movies, reading sources, and writing down ideas in order to make informed decisions about their topics. It takes diligence and dedication to move from the story treatment to the final draft of a script, as it entails a fair amount of editing to make sure the dialogues, characters, locations, type of shots, and camera movements all fit together into a meaningful whole (popular filmmaker Quentin Tarantino spent over a decade writing the film script for *Inglourious Basterds*!).

Why Call It Research?

There are good reasons for embracing the term research with regard to the process of making a movie, as we seek a place for film as a discipline within the undergraduate research movement. As colleges and universities have placed an increasing amount of emphasis on high-impact educational practices such as undergraduate research, film majors risk losing out on central funding for research and in the race for recognition at film festivals and award ceremonies by not participating as fully as possible in academic research endeavors. Hence, the need to clarify the reasons why academia should consider the filmmaking process as original, impactful research.

Perhaps the most obvious way for film students to engage in undergraduate research is to collaborate with faculty members in scientific and social studies disciplines, which have been endorsing the involvement of undergraduates in collaborative research for quite a while. By researching a film subject from an interdisciplinary perspective, undergraduate students will expand and deepen their understanding of cinematic representation and its impact on human behavior and society, contributing to the film and media studies scholarship in novel ways. For example, by performing a neuroscientific study of the influence of diverse editing rhythms on the spectator's brain, film students have a broader comprehension of the ways in which films may affect human behavior, making better-informed decisions when producing their own movies.

Producing a movie in the digital age also requires a solid grasp of computer skills since films have increasingly become digital creations. Currently, films are mainly shot with digital video cameras, edited on a computer using software such as Adobe Premiere, Final Cut Pro, or Avid, enhanced with digital visual and special effects, retrieved from drives at movie theaters and streamed to television, computer, or iPhone screens. Developing and maintaining digital literacy by either enrolling in computer training classes or by working alongside a computer science professor is therefore essential for film students. Furthermore, producing a film entails creative abilities in other arts disciplines such as theater studies (in order to learn how to design costumes and sets) and musical studies (for the purpose of composing music and recording sound). Film students can highly benefit from being able to create the audio portion of their own films as they can get around the issue of copyrighted music/audio and fully bring their artistic vision to life.

Another reason why we should call the process of filmmaking itself research is that, much like the process of scientific inquiry, it is a method of discovery. Films tend, in fact, to evolve in unpredictable and significant ways through the creative process of their production. Hence, the importance of keeping thorough and detailed notes during all the stages of film production as a point of departure for critically reflecting on the specific thematic, aesthetic, and formal choices made along the way. Undergraduate students should never underestimate the importance of note-taking during film production because it forces them to engage deeply with the material, and to become aware of the decision-making process, especially when it generates totally unexpected outcomes.

All of the above proves the breadth and depth of both interdisciplinary knowledge and technical skills required for making a film informed by well-researched and developed ideas.

How to Document the Process

To properly consider the filmmaking process as rigorous undergraduate research, film students need to document and reflect on it, just as a visual artist does in a statement accompanying an exhibition. This allows the casual spectator to understand how film undergraduates inquire about a topic and create their work, including how they conduct background research on a particular film subject, what techniques they use in film production, and why they edit shots, scenes, and sequences in a certain way. The documentation process varies depending on the type of film project. For example, a film assignment could culminate in an artist statement accompanying a screening that critically reflects on the stages of film production, or in a handout explaining the research process used to create an audiovisual essay. Independently of the type of film project, the most important part of the documentation process is to explain the kind of research conducted, the creative decisions made, the various stages of development, and the ways that the film project achieved (or did not) the intended goals.

Taking into consideration the fact that evaluating a film project has a significant subjective component, criteria should include not only quality of the final product but a clear demonstration and documentation of the iterative process involved from start to finish. Not only is understanding and mastering the filmmaking process an important lesson for undergraduate students, it also allows the professor to better mentor them, becoming familiar with some of the thought processes behind the decisions students made. This mentoring relationship is one of the hallmarks of undergraduate research in most fields, and one of the things that makes it so worthwhile and high impact in academia.

Sample of Filmmaking Artistic Statements

FILMMAKING ARTISTIC STATEMENT BY RAUNAK KAPOOR

University of North Carolina, School of Filmmaking 1533 South Main St. Winston-Salem, NC 27127–2738

I have always been the sort of child, who, instead of directly following the steps he was given, would try to explore different ways of doing it. The sort of child who would try to give everything he did a unique style. Once, when I was in 4th grade, our computer teacher asked us to draw a square in LOGO, an instructional programming language used for drawing. Even though we were asked to follow the steps in the book to make a square, I wanted to explore what more I could create. I used squares as my primary structures and created a house with a tree besides it in the time it took others to complete the square. This impressed my teachers and my work was shown to the principal, who for my work, gave me a chocolate. This was probably the first time I had taken an unconventional approach, which has since this day been an integral part of all my work.

When you live in a country like India, everyone expects you to follow one of the three professions; engineer, doctor, or lawyer. Here, ever since you are born, you are carried into a world of pre-established beliefs and outdated stereotypes, where every member of the society has something to say about your actions. Living in such a society and my deep hatred for studying political sciences and human biology, I grew up believing that I would become a computer engineer and took up science in high school.

I had never liked science much and during high school, reading novels, looking at photographs, watching movies and playing games became my escape from the monotonous daily routine of studying. I realized I get very fascinated by stories. They gave me an insight into different aspects of life and introduced me to new worlds. Just as asserted in the famous quote from the movie *Dead poet's society*, "Medicine, law, business, engineering, these are noble pursuits and necessary to sustain life. But poetry, beauty, romance, love, these are what we stay alive for", I realized that stories, experiences, and memories are what gives our lives meaning. This love for stories over time also became a breakthrough in the whole mystery of my career path.

On exploring different ways of doing something with my newfound interest in storytelling, I found out that I was not much interested in the contemporary methods of telling stories of writing blogs, novels or articles. I wanted to tell stories in a way that my stories immediately connected with someone's soul. In my search, I found that visuals are the best way for people to relate with, feel, learn, and consume. A picture can tell you a whole story worth a thousand words, in a single frame. I started exploring photography and film making as art using a borrowed camera and under the guidance of my uncle, a professional photographer in India, for most of my senior year in high school and learnt through my own experiences.

I developed my own rights and wrongs, techniques and aesthetics. I started loving to shoot black and white as I felt that, by taking the colors out of a picture, I could focus more on the story, composition, light and the emotions of my subjects. I also realized I could show more of the story through the background than the foreground and started focusing on always getting a perfect background. Also by shooting regularly, I have become better at spotting stories, placing subjects creatively, chasing the light, making quick decisions, using slow shutter creatively, using the distortion in the wide angle lenses to give drama in street portraits, exploring unique perspectives and compositions, using different lenses, etc.

I try to give all my work a unique story. My work revolves mostly around street, travel, and portraiture, and is full of stories that I find deeply moving, encouraging or motivational. My photo story, "the leaders" provides an insight into the various types of societies in India. It was a project that helped me learn about different cultures, befriend various people and gather many new experiences and memories. Even though it was my first photo project, it was an important story I wished to share with the world. It encouraged me to start sharing my stories and gain confidence in my skills and style as a photographer. My second photo story, "joy in a puddle of mud" was inspired by a simple idea, that every child deserves education irrespective of their background. Education can be the means to liberate these young souls from a vicious circle that has forced their forefathers into petty jobs and a life of poverty. I collaborated with "Harmony house", an NGO aimed towards providing basic education and support for such youth. I traveled around Delhi and connected with families and children belonging to many different backgrounds. I observed that one thing each child, entrapped in poverty, had in common was the "will of fire", an ambition to one-day matter in this vast world. This photo story was a call for help for these children. My third photo story, "life in Old Delhi", was inspired by the priceless moments and memories I gathered, traveling in narrow, dingy lanes, of old Delhi, which, once the most famous place in India, has now become an overcrowded place housing people from all cultures and economic strata. In its narrow lanes, I saw and captured the most beautiful moments of both joy and sorrow. My first short film, "A letter to the past" was a manifestation of a desire deep inside everyone's heart; a desire to see what would happen differently if you could change your past. Giving such stories life through my films and photography is what I thrive for as an artist.

In more than one way, the art of photography and filmmaking has helped me redeem the control of my life. It has given me enough strength to break the barriers of my society and follow an unconventional path. It has encouraged me to go out and explore the world with my own eyes, observe its rare beauty, capture its various stories and understand its deepest sufferings. My ambition is to become a respected photographer and filmmaker so that I can share my stories with the entire world. I want to be free of limitations, learn and produce work. My art motivates me and gives me the passion for following this ambition.

FILMMAKING ARTISTIC STATEMENT BY ERIC D. HOWELL

2015 Mcknight Fellows in Media Arts

http://myfilmnorth.org/wp-content/uploads/2015/12/2015-Artist-Statements.pdf

Slice-of-life stories do not interest me. Cinematic journeys with cathartic experiences and empathetic characters are what I yearn for.

My films use surrealistic settings with a large scope to open the imagination and ignite the curiosity of an audience. My characters have small, relatable stories with authentic moral dilemmas that play in contrast to that scale. The effect of this allows viewers to "escape" and let their guard down, which in turn allows me to open them to ideas and emotions. *In short, I take people far-far-away to look at themselves up close.* This sets my films apart from parochial cinema, and propels them to play on a global stage. Film is mass-media and is therefore most effective when it reaches a mass audience to elicit a collective catharsis.

My approach requires a unique skill set that includes experience with professional actors, ability to lead large crews, technical aptitude, expertise in screenwriting, and an understanding of the industry. Having recently completed production of my first feature film, my career is primed to reach a new level.

The first influence towards this aesthetic came as a young boy. While not the best film I've ever seen, *Close Encounters of the Third Kind* made a significant impression at just the right time. It was the first film that made me "gasp". My limited cinematic experiences had me believe that these aliens would do harm as they passed over Devil's Tower. Then the movie shifts our empathy and communicates with us in the only way that makes sense—music. Because of this scope and spectacle my imagination had been opened. My empathy for the characters peaked and the story became indelible.

Charlie Chaplin's approach is one that I share; The use of dialogue in cinema is a failure of visual storytelling. Hitchcock's use of juxtaposition exemplifies what can be done to create the "third idea". Show a banana peel, show a man walking, show a banana peel. The idea of the man slipping is created in the mind of the audience. The more "third ideas" the better the film.

Currently, my films exist on the border between realism and surrealism. Cinematography, sound, and music work to create a recognizable but mysterious world. This design forces the audience to attach to something familiar—a character experiencing a moral dilemma. This is not a new concept, but my world view and aesthetic make it unique. Rather than quantifying this in words, I prefer to let the work speak for itself.

Documentary films commonly use sympathy to make a political or social comment. Through empathy my audience experiences a journey as if in a first-person perspective. The emotions of the protagonists become the emotions of the audience. The ideas I'm proposing become ideas created in the minds of the audience as if they were their own.

Recognizable characters experiencing life in large scale settings. Through this "escapism" approach I am able to engage, entertain, and inform so that my work may be seen by a mass audience. With over twenty-years of experience in every aspect of film production, my career is now at a tipping point to reach a higher level.

Conclusion

When film undergraduate students are deliberate about the various stages of the filmmaking process, seriously engaged in interdisciplinary work, and well informed on current film studies debates, they are performing rigorous academic research. This rigor is crucial because it encourages scholars in other fields to look at film projects as academically sound inquiry procedures, having the effect of increasing credibility and respect from professors and researchers in other parts of the academy.

Questions for Discussion

- Could your film project be community-based, and if so, how?
- Could your film project be socially engaged, and if so, how?
- When is filmmaking really not research?
- Why do some filmmakers succeed with a very small research component?
- Should all senior film projects have a research component?

References

Kapoor, R. (2019). Filmmaking artistic statement. Retrieved from www.uncsa.edu/admissions/how-to-write-an-artistic-statement/filmmaking-artistic-statement-example.aspx.

Kurosawa, A. (1983). *Something like an autobiography*. New York: Vintage Books.

10

INTERDISCIPLINARY IDEAS

The Path Less Taken

Interdisciplinarity in general is based on the deep affinity of all branches of knowledge, an affinity which is best expressed in philosophical thought. Art and philosophy have a common purpose: to change the inner human being, but they go about this purpose differently. Philosophy addresses the inner person in us directly, through conceptual thinking, while art transforms external reality—everything from landscape to the human body itself—in order to transform the human person's inner world. The various art forms are united by this common task and way of doing things and therefore are best understood in their mutual conjunction. This idea forms the basis for the simultaneous study of several art forms, as well as of philosophy along with the arts.

Vladimir Marchenkov

Archaically, discipline meant instruction given to a disciple, and a "disciple" would take apart. Meanings for the prefix "inter" include between, among, and together. The word interdisciplinary as a whole suggests learning by both taking apart and bringing together. Interdisciplinary research is indeed vast with boundaries in flux that we continue to tailor to meet our own interests and contexts of study.

Andrea Frohne

Breakthrough innovation occurs when we bring down boundaries and encourage disciplines to learn from each other.

Gyan Nagpal

Summary

This chapter will open with an explanation of the reasons why some of the most exciting discoveries in recent times have occurred at the intersections of traditional disciplines, pointing to the lack of extensive research linking film with other disciplinary fields and, thus, to the possibility for students of making original contributions to knowledge by tackling interdisciplinary subjects. This discussion will be followed by examples of successful interdisciplinary undergraduate research seminars and projects and by suggestions for possible topics. The conclusion will show the benefits many students and professors have enjoyed from such collaborations, providing samples of student projects from journals and conferences.

Why Two Different Disciplines?

The Survey Report from the 2016 annual meeting of the Global Research Council states "There is a wealth of literature arguing the important role interdisciplinary research has to play, particularly in addressing complex and societal challenges" (Gleed & Marchant, 2016). There is an increasing emphasis on finding solutions to some of these complex problems, or at least discussing ways they might be solved, in undergraduate curricula. In a recent article entitled "Pushing the Frontiers of Interdisciplinary Research: An Idea Whose Time has Come" there is a description of the bold initiatives at Stanford University and UC Berkeley that bring faculty together from different disciplines to aid in the discovery of knowledge (Gershon, 2000).

One fascinating example of interdisciplinary discovery in audiovisual technology is the design of camera lenses and computers screens' antireflective surfaces inspired by observing the structure of cicadas', dragonflies', and butterflies' wings (Han et al., 2016; Siddique, Gomard & Hölscher, 2015). By reproducing the random nanostructure found on the surface of these insects' wings, scientists determined that it is possible to eliminate the display glare typical of computer screens, iPads, camera lenses, and smartphones. This is described in the article "Bio-Inspired Functional Surfaces Based on Laser-Induced Periodic Surface Structures," published in *Materials*, a peer-reviewed open- access journal of materials science and engineering (Müller, Kunz, & Gräf, 2016). The article (www.mdpi.com/1996-1944/9/6/476/htm) describes how the natural world offers ingenious solutions to solve technical problems related to material surfaces.

One of the biggest challenges in undergraduate research is finding a project that has not been done before. While faculty do not expect undergraduates to make significant contributions to a given discipline, they do find importance in the originality of this work, not simply repeating a study that is new to the student. To that end, choosing a project that examines an aspect of a discipline from the perspective of another discipline enables students to find topics not previously exhausted or explored in great depth. Many different subject areas in film intersect well with other disciplines. For example, we naturally tend to pairing film with disciplines such as anthropology, music, theater, photography, art, language, literature, and sociology, though less obvious ones such as biology, physics, and medicine can be quite interesting. As outlined below, undergraduate seminars linking film with architecture, film with history, and film with education have also proved to be fruitful pairs.

The Housing First Village Project: A Collaboration between Film, Architecture, and Community Partners (Bozeman, MT)

The result of a partnership among the Human Resources Development Center, Reverend Connie Campbell-Pearson, and the Schools of Architecture and Film & Photography at MSU (Montana State University), the Housing First Village Project (HFV) is intended to provide transformative housing to Bozeman's chronically homeless. Targeted towards the homeless population that is most at risk, HFV is a safe and sustainable model designed to support successful reintegration into community living and permanent housing. The single-user "tiny" homes or shelters would provide a cost-effective way to address the growing issue of homelessness, while maintaining the autonomy and dignity of the resident. Utilizing best practices from around the nation, this model is based on the "Housing First" philosophy, which limits the barriers to entry and provides supportive services to residents for mental health and addiction counseling.

In May 2017, architecture students and community volunteers began the construction of a prototype tiny house under the supervision of architecture professors Ralph Johnson and Bill Clinton (School of Architecture, MSU). Every step in the building process has been thoroughly documented by film students Jessica Portuondo and Evangeline Koonce with the guidance and supervision of film professor Lucia Ricciardelli (School of Film & Photography, MSU). The outcome of this filming was the production of *Seeking Shelter: A Tiny Home Solution*, a documentary short about the HFV Project. The documentary film mixes observational footage showing architecture graduate students and volunteers building a Tiny House Prototype for the HFV Project with interviews of some of the project main players discussing the beneficial impact of the Housing First Village initiative on the Bozeman community and, especially, on Montana's homeless population (see Figure 10.1). Homelessness is an unacceptable condition in a country of our wealth. *Seeking Shelter* demonstrates how every community can build a village where the residents feel protected, respected, and connected. By breaking down stereotypes about homelessness, the documentary film will hopefully help lower the walls of hatred and fear that so often lead to discrimination, isolation, and exclusion.

The Digital Storywork Partnership: A Cross-Cultural and Interdisciplinary Collaboration

The Digital Storywork Partnership (DSP) is an ongoing interdisciplinary project that integrates community-based participatory research (CBPR) with Indigenous Research Methodologies (IRMs) to advance historical and cultural

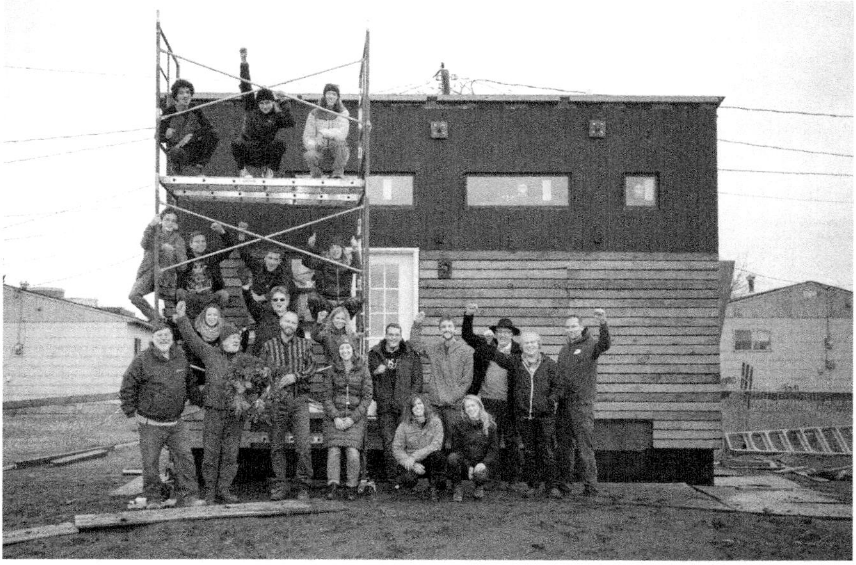

FIGURE 10.1 Film and architecture students and faculty (MSU) and community partners in front of a Tiny House Prototype (December 2017). © Shelly Saunders.

understanding, elevate indigenous philosophies within research and filmmaking, and promote educational self-determination. Co-researchers hail from a variety of Nations, including the Piikani (Blackfeet), Apsáalooke (Crow), and Little Shell. Partners include indigenous youth and educators; community nonprofits; MSU and tribal college students, faculty, and alumni; and elders, language teachers, and tribal leaders. The DSP process has been emphasizing: (1) the identification of community research interests, cultural protocol needs, and methodological, technical, and creative recommendations; and (2) the application of appropriate methods to investigate community interests. The DSP

- provides a strengths-based model to share community knowledges in culturally revitalizing ways;
- produces counter-narratives to challenge Eurocentric knowledges (e.g., curricula, documentary films, etc.);
- engages community members as co-researchers throughout the knowledge production process;
- promotes tribal self-determination within research and education;
- provides professional development for indigenous filmmakers, researchers, and teachers;
- expands community access to equipment and technical skills;

- teaches students and faculty about cultural protocol;
- supports cross-cultural and intergenerational learning.

Launched in the spring of 2015 by MSU professors Lucia Ricciardelli (School of Film & Photography) and Christine Rogers Stanton (Education Department), the DSP project has led to the development of a series of documentary workshops that have engaged Blackfeet Community College (BCC), Buffalo Hide Academy, Plenty Coups High School, and MSU students and faculty in the creation of audiovisual counter-narratives (2015—today). Ricciardelli and Stanton's goal has been to promote intercultural partnership and mentorship while developing young Native American documentary filmmakers. Over the past three years, they have produced four publications (three book chapters and one article) and given several presentations at national and international conferences on the results of their collaboration with the Piikani community. It is noteworthy that Ricciardelli and Stanton presented the DSP project with two undergraduate students from BCC at the Days of the Piikani Community Showcase (September 21–24, 2015) in Browning, MT (see Figure 10.2) and at the Annual Convention of the American Educational Research Association (April 8–12, 2016) in Washington, DC.

Documentary Filmmaking and the Crisis of Eurocentric History

This film seminar enrolled 12 film majors from MSU and nine Native American students from BCC, examining the contemporary Western crisis of Eurocentric history through the lens of documentary filmmaking. By addressing the ways in which the disciplines of film and media studies, postcolonial theory, and postmodernism have engaged with the notions of reality, documentary evidence, and historical narrative, the course addressed the central questions: What type of knowledge validates evidential uses of the photographic archive in the digital age? How have the postmodern collapse of meta-narratives, the

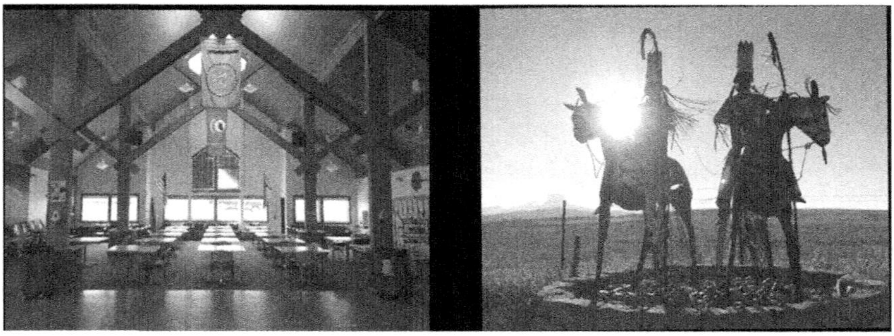

FIGURE 10.2 Blackfeet Community College, Piikani Nation (Browning, MT).

postcolonial critique of historicism, and the advent of digitization operated to subvert the ways in which documentary form is now conceived? In what ways could audiovisual historical narratives support personal experience and express cultural differences? Can contemporary documentary filmmaking contribute to endorse a collective dynamic in which idiosyncratic expression resists incorporation into a totalizing official discourse?

The seminar was designed to give students the critical tools necessary to describe and evaluate the documentary film as an audiovisual form of historical narration. In investigating the concept of visual "truth" against a background of diminished public confidence in the "objectivity" of the camera, the course was intended to make students reflect on the modes and functions of history in the era of digitization. By the end of the course, students were able to develop:

- The ability to investigate the subjects of photographic evidence and historical narration from an interdisciplinary perspective;
- the ability to argue for some possible causes that led to the contemporary Western crisis in Eurocentric history;
- the ability to create an audiovisual historical narrative and reflect on its own production;
- the ability to evaluate the impact of historical narration on the construction of cultural identity;
- the ability to engage cross-culturally: to embrace an active, two-way process of communicating with and learning from another culture. The two cultures involved in this course were BCC students and faculty and MSU students and faculty (see Figure 10.3).

Suggestions for Possible Interdisciplinary Seminars Involving Film

There are many possibilities for similar undergraduate research seminars such as courses that:

- Link film history, art history, and music history to trace the development of specific stylistic trends in a chosen film industry;
- examine the similarities and differences between film language and natural language using Christian Metz's (1974) semiological study of cinema;
- analyze the main tenets of realism in art by comparing mid-1800 French painting to 1930s British documentary filmmaking;
- design and produce original soundtrack for student films in collaboration with music students;
- research technological innovations in film equipment that have been inspired from biology;

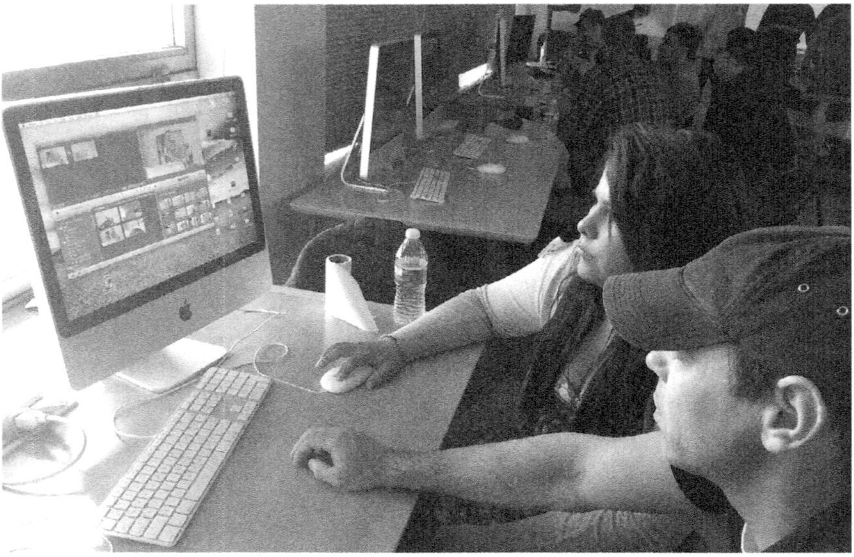

FIGURE 10.3 MSU and BCC students and faculty working on collaborative documentary projects (Spring 2015).

- apply indigenous methodologies to the study of Hollywood-inspired storytelling approaches.

An interesting exercise, either alone or in a group, is to come up with as many interdisciplinary seminars as possible that might work, and then try to come up with one or two that would not work. The second part of that exercise is tougher than one might think. This could be done in class with the students divided up into teams.

Sample Abstracts Submitted to NCUR (National Conference on Undergarduate Research)

www.cur.org/conferences_and_events/student_events/ncur/archive/

THE EVOLUTION OF SOUNDTRACK IN CIVIL WAR FILM

Andy Deen (Jack Ryan), Department of Interdisciplinary Studies, Gettysburg College, Gettysburg, Pennsylvania

The Civil War film genre has long relied on music to invoke emotion and provide thematic continuity. Although the earliest silent films about the Civil War lacked pre-recorded sound, most movie halls provided live accompaniment in the form of a pianist or small orchestra. The 1915 premiere of *Birth of a Nation* was revolutionary: for the first time, a film director was personally involved in the compilation of the orchestral score used to accompany the film. The introduction of synchronized, pre-recorded sound helped solidify the musical conventions then emerging within the genre. One of these trends was the use of pre-existing Civil War melodies to establish historical setting. The role of period music in the Civil War film genre continues to expand. Although early film composers wrote exclusively for the symphonic orchestra, present-day composers often include "authentic" period music ensembles like the fife and drum corps. As period music becomes a staple feature of the genre, film composers and directors must decide how best to integrate originally composed music with pre-existing Civil War melodies. Filmmakers are confronted with other artistic challenges, including the intersection of diegetic music (music whose source is visible on screen) and non-diegetic music (off-screen music like a symphonic soundtrack), and the concept of musical authenticity. Some recent films challenge the traditional scoring conventions of the genre by using music in innovative ways. This interdisciplinary presentation will synthesize film studies, music performance, and Civil War history. Topics to be addressed include the emergence of period music, the relationship between diegetic and non-diegetic sound, and the recent integration of film score and period music. Film clips from *Glory, Gettysburg*, and *Gods and Generals* will provide examples and illustrations.

PREJUDICE IN JURY TRIALS: REPRESENTATIONS OF LAW IN LITERATURE AND FILM

Author: Michael Bavalsky Faculty Mentor: Jenny Kijowski Department: History Institution: Macaulay Honors College at Brooklyn College Address: 35 West 67th Street New York, NY 10,023

In my paper, I will be analyzing fictional depictions of jury trials, with a focus on the prejudices espoused by some jury members and how those prejudices influence their verdict. I will focus primarily on jury trials as they are depicted in three specific publications: Harper Lee's *To Kill a Mockingbird* (1960), Jerome Lawrence and Robert Edwin Lee's *Inherit the Wind* (1955), and Reginald Rose's *Twelve Angry Men* (1957). *To Kill a Mockingbird* focuses on issues of racial discrimination in 1930s Alabama, *Inherit the Wind* is a fictional depiction of the Scopes Monkey Trial, while *Twelve Angry Men* offers a glimpse into the minds of jury members as they deliberate on a case in which an adolescent from a disadvantaged background is charged with murdering his father in a fit of rage. Significantly, all three of these literary works were published within a five-year period. The mid-to-late 20th century was a time when United States law and culture gradually began to shift away from racial inequality, as evidenced by the Supreme Court's landmark ruling in Brown v. Board of Education, as well as other historical events that bespoke a move in the direction of a more egalitarian and just society. My paper will consider the above-mentioned works in their historical and cultural context, and evaluate what the authors suggest about the feasibility of a minority defendant obtaining an impartial jury—i.e., whether it is possible for a jury to be verily unbiased and dispassionate in considering a case, or if it is inevitable that a jury's verdict will be influenced by the personal beliefs and dispositions of its members.

EXPLORING PRECIOUS METAL MINING IN PERU THROUGH FILM

Author: Madi Sachs Faculty mentor: Professor Andrew Snustad Department of Foreign Languages and Literature University of Minnesota Duluth 1049 University Drive Duluth, MN 55812

Precious metal mining in Peru has been an extremely controversial issue for hundreds of years, largely due to the variable distribution of wealth produced and the environmental implications. Although mining and the problems associated with it have been in Peru for centuries, in recent years Peru has become increasingly attractive for the growing number of international businesses, including mining companies, due to its natural wealth and unsaturated markets. This demands that fair and sustainable business practices are firmly established in order to insure the wellbeing not only of Peru as a nation but also to its rural community members who are oftentimes most negatively affected by mining. These community members have faced relocation, unfulfilled promises, and serious health effects despite being represented by their government and even talking directly to the mining companies. This is forcing rural people in mining areas to search for different outlets to have their voices heard. Film has progressively become a popular vehicle to do this, and critical analyses of these films help reveal the root issues related to mining. The films analyzed in this paper are all produced in Spanish, filmed in Peru, and include locals. *En el corazón de Conga*, the documentary focused on most, was produced in 2012, and it includes in-depth interviews with the local people of Cajamarca who are affected by the Conga mine. *Molinopampa* is a short film that illustrates how damaging mining-related water contamination would be for one local community. Finally, *La hija de la laguna* reveals the intense effort an Andean community puts forth to stop the local mine. By directly exploring mining issues through film, the medium local Peruvians are utilizing, an authentic perspective is revealed, and the people's messages are echoed to new audiences.

Conclusion

Interdisciplinary study is not only mind-expanding and fascinating, it is also becoming increasingly common in many more academic fields than it has been in the past. Choosing to embrace an interdisciplinary approach to research projects involving film can provide students a less trodden path on which to make discoveries, an avenue for creative expression, and a chance to add something meaningful and original to the current body of knowledge. Given the emphasis on interdisciplinary research in the 21st century, it also prepares students for a world in which collaboration and the interdependence of scholars are paramount.

Questions for Discussion

- What might be some discipline pairings worth exploring?
- Are there any discipline pairings that would NOT work as an interdisciplinary seminar?
- Does this chapter generate new ideas based on interdisciplinarity?
- Why is integrating interdisciplinary subjects into film research important?

References

Frohne, A. (2019). Interdisciplinarity defined. *Ohio University College of Fine Arts, para 8*. Retrieved from www.ohio.edu/finearts/interarts/about/interdisciplinarity.cfm.

Gershon, D. (2000). Pushing the frontiers of interdisciplinary research: An idea whose time has come. *Nature*, *404*(6775): 313–315. doi:10.1038/35005213.

Gleed, A., & Marchant, D. (2016). Interdisciplinarity: Survey report for the Global Research Council. Retrieved from www.globalresearchcouncil.org/sites/default/files/pdfs/Interdisciplinarity%20Report%20for%20GRC_DJS%20Research.pdf.

Han, Z. W., Wang, Z., Feng, X. M., Li, B., Mu, Z. Z., Zhang, J. Q., … Ren, L. Q. (2016). Antireflective surface inspired from biology: A review. *Biosurface and Biotribology*, *2*(4): 121–192.

Marchenkov, V. (2019). Interdisciplinarity defined. *Ohio University College of Fine Arts, para 11*. Retrieved from www.ohio.edu/finearts/interarts/about/interdisciplinarity.cfm.

Metz, C. (1974). *Film language: A semiotics of the cinema*. New York: Oxford University Press.

Müller, F., Kunz, C., & Gräf, S. (2016). Bio-inspired functional surfaces based on laser-induced periodic surface structures. *Materials*, *9*(6): 476.

Nagpal, G. (2013). *Talent economics: The fine line between winning and losing the global war for talent*. London: Kogan Page. Retrieved from www.arabinnovation.net/ainac16.html.

Siddique, R. H., Gomard, G., & Hölscher, H. (2015). The role of random nanostructures for the omnidirectional anti-reflection properties of the glasswing butterfly. *Nature Communications*, *6*(1): 6909. doi:10.1038/ncomms7909.

11

THE DISCOVERY OF KNOWLEDGE IN FILM HISTORY

> History is always written wrong, and so always needs to be rewritten.
>
> George Santayana

> Historiography [is] the study of the way history has been and is written–the history of historical writing ... When you study "historiography" you do not study the events of the past directly, but the changing interpretations of those events in the works of individual historians.
>
> Conal Furay and Michael J. Salevouris

> Historians are prophets with their face turned backward.
>
> Friedrich von Schlegel

Summary

As part of their degree requirements, undergraduate students enrolled in film programs are usually expected to write a handful of film history essays, specifying their topic of historical inquiry in a proposal inclusive of annotated bibliography. On occasion, film undergraduates are asked to narrow down their film topics by writing a literature review, and, only rarely, they are exposed to other possibilities for original work such as producing oral histories and audiovisual essays dealing with film history. This chapter will review the process for film historical research contextualizing it for the undergraduate student population. Suggested topics in film history will be outlined followed by sample abstracts and questions for discussion.

Introduction

The teaching of film history courses in colleges and universities and the recognition of the value of film as an area of "serious" academic research are fairly new phenomena dating back to the 1960s. This means that film history is a ripe subject for research and, thus, that undergraduate students can contribute to expand this field of knowledge.

Before undertaking specific topics in film history, it is critical to introduce undergraduate students to the concept of historiography: the process of selection, arrangement, and interpretation through which films, institutions, people, events, and discourses are shaped into the body of knowledge we call "film history." What does it mean to organize knowledge from a historical perspective? How do we decide what part of the past is worthy of our attention? What kind of questions do we want to ask about the past? What are the differences among the aesthetic, technological, social, and economic approach to film history? How do we frame them differently?

By becoming familiar with some of the major contemporary historiographical debates, students realize that the writing of history is not the passive transmission of facts but rather an active process of judgment. They learn that the very selection of what events are worthy of being chronicled and the ordering of those events into a narrative sequence are both acts of interpretation and, thus, that the film historian is not presenting the indisputable "truth" about the past but, rather, an argument as to how a particular event might have happened. This chapter is designed to help undergraduate students understand the process of historical research and narrow down topic areas in film history, suggesting small projects that have not been done before. This allows film students to make original contributions and thereby enhance the discipline, albeit in a small way. Whether it is an independent project with a topic chosen by the student or a small component of a film professor's larger research program, it is important to follow the process appropriate to the discipline that is followed by film historians everywhere.

Reasons for Researching Film History

Researching the history of film is a daunting and time-consuming task, so why do it? First of all, it helps you recognize that many contemporary films have been inspired and informed by prior masterworks. For example, Alfonso Cuarón's *Roma* (2018), based on the filmmaker's own childhood in early 1970s Mexico City, borrows many of the stylistic conventions and thematic concerns of Italian neorealism with its use of non-professional actors alongside professionals and improvisation to obtain more naturalistic performances. Roberto Rossellini's *Roma, città aperta* (*Rome, Open City*, 1945) and Vittorio De Sica's *Ladri di biciclette* (*Bicycle Thieves*, 1947) are two of the neorealist masterpieces that clearly influenced Cuarón's filmmaking approach in *Roma.* This stylistic and thematic similarity can provide undergraduate students with a unique opportunity to study the history of neorealism across national boundaries and different time periods.

Examining the history of cinema allows students to better understand contemporary filmmaking practices so that they can make more informed decisions about their film productions. We often say that "history repeats itself"; yet, if you analyze the successes and failures of the past, you can learn how to avoid repeating the same mistakes in the future. More important, researching the past not only can provide you with insight into your culture of origin, it also can give you access to another culture's worldview, contributing to the increase of cross-cultural awareness. By watching foreign films and researching the processes of their production, for example, you can gain insights about a different culture's film industry, belief system, and customs, expanding your knowledge of human behavior, cinematic language, and diverse production management approaches. In the end, history is nearly always a reflection on the past from the perspective of the present; which means, historical thinking can be a key to understanding yourself, your culture, and alternative ways of living. This increased awareness is paramount to developing believable characters and compelling stories.

Process: Bringing Film History Alive in Novel Ways

Before deciding on a topic for original research, undergraduate students should study the literature in their chosen subject area of film history. This might involve typing topics into Google Scholar, their university's library online catalogue, or other databases and then critically examining the sources and the content. Be mindful that Wikipedia is not a reliable source of information, although sometimes the articles can have good sources cited in their bibliographies. Websites such as NCUR (National Council on Undergraduate Research), BCUR (British Conference of Undergraduate Research), ACUR (Australian Conference of Undergraduate Research), and JUR (Journal of Undergraduate Research) from Colorado State University, can provide examples of completed undergraduate research in film history. Many resources are available, including interlibrary loans and the online resources that are annotated in Chapter 17. When narrowing and finalizing the topic, be sure to consult your professor and have a look back at Chapter 3, Choosing Film Topics and Formulating Appropriate Research Questions, to fully understand the complexity of this initial phase of research.

Besides choosing a research topic and performing a literature search on the chosen subject, writing a research paper in film history involves a particular set of abilities such as finding and evaluating archival data, selecting what type of historical approach to use (whether aesthetic, technological, economic, or social), conceptualizing a thesis statement, developing a paper proposal inclusive of annotated bibliography, and selecting an academic citation style. The internet has provided film studies students with a vast array of essay-writing tools and services, rendering the task of writing an academic paper easier than ever. Several of these sources are listed in Chapter 17 for your perusal. You can find a list of possible essay topics in film history as follows.

Possible Research Topics in Film History

- The filmic construction of national identity in early European cinema (1890s–1919).
- Soviet montage's challenge to mainstream filmmaking chronological narrative structure.
- European cinema in the 1920s: French Impressionism vis-à-vis German Expressionism.
- The international development of sound cinema: language and national identity.
- The nationalization of the German film industry (1930s–1940s).
- The far-reaching influence of Italian neorealism.
- The Americanization of Japanese culture: Japanese cinema under the American Occupation (1945–1952).
- Authorship and the growth of the art cinema: personal style vis-à-vis national style.
- The (French) *Nouvelle Vague*: an enduring challenge to the Hollywood style of filmmaking.
- Great Britain: kitchen-sink cinema.
- The Italian Spaghetti Western: a transnational genre?
- New German Cinema: historical trauma and national identity.
- Brazil: *Cinema Novo*.
- The Japanese New Wave.
- Political filmmaking in the Third World (1960s–1970s).
- The Dogme 95 movement.
- Oceanian cinema: aboriginal cultures and the white man.
- Cinema in the digital age: towards a global film culture.
- The development of special effects technologies in cinema: from Georges Méliès to James Cameron.
- Transnational comparison between Great Britain and Japan and their conversion to sound-film production.
- Discuss how globalization has helped promote stronger ties among different national film industries.
- Interview and/or write about local and/or lesser-known filmmakers.
- Conduct and/or examine oral and written histories.

- Research old movie cameras and new practices with that equipment.
- Explore the history of different film cultures in your region.
- Trace the history of female film editors in the United States.
- Interview a film history professor about his/her research area.
- Compare and contrast two or more film history textbooks. What eras/filmmakers does each book emphasize?

Sample Abstracts Submitted to NCUR

www.cur.org/conferences_and_events/student_events/ncur/archive/

SEX, CINEMA, AND CENSORSHIP: A HISTORICAL SURVEY OF CENSORSHIP OF SEX IN FILM

Brandon S. Jordan (John A. Duvall) Department of Communications, Dominican University of California, San Rafael, CA 94901

Almost since the inception of film-making as a medium of expression it has come under intense scrutiny for its use of violence and sex, and in contemporary films sex more so than violence. Whether it was the Production Code, the Legion of Decency, or even the now existing Motion Picture Association of America, movies have been the targets of censorship. At first, the idea of censorship is that it was a voluntary "self-censor" agreement between producers and the studios. Now a rating system tells the viewer what they will watch, and more importantly what they are able to watch. Over time this idea has become so ingrained into the business of movie making, that even if, in the modern sense, an "NC-17" rated film is produced it won't play in a theater. I hope to explore the legal issues involved in rating films, what constitutes censorship, and in doing so illustrate the ethics involved in censoring art. I will develop a historical context, analyze a sampling of "controversial" films and their legal implications from the 1930's to present time, and discuss past and current systems of ratings and censorship.

ONLY THE STRONG SURVIVE: BLAXPLOITATION AND THE CIVIL RIGHTS MOVEMENT

Author: Anthony Bennett Advisor: Carolina Conte Department of Film Jacksonville University 2800 University Blvd N Jacksonville, FL 32211

The tropes are as memorable now as they were scandalous then: the unrepentant pimp, the subservient and enthusiastic prostitute, the unrepentantly evil (and invariably white) authority figure. Two hours of sex, explosions and ludicrous dialogue later, the hero would stand victorious, off to whatever nefarious deeds masquerading as noble ones. Such was blaxploitation, the hugely popular 1970s movement of urban-oriented dramas designed largely to cash in on the heretofore-overlooked African-American audience. The genre was as popular with

African-American audiences as it was reviled by their traditional leadership organizations (blaxploitation was itself coined by then-NAACP president Junius Griffin). But why did this dichotomy exist? Were African-American audiences simply responding to seeing their own depicted positively, whatever their onscreen pursuits? Or did the need for these characters to pursue their own ends reflect on the performance of the aforementioned organizations? My research is a look at the genre of blaxploitation from its beginnings to its decline, as well as the complicated post-1960s developments in the African-American Civil Rights Movement that preceded blaxploitation and in some cases engendered themes in its more resonant work. I intend to show within a scholastic framework that blaxploitation was not a betrayal of the empowering effects of the Civil Rights Movement but a response to its stagnation, which gave African-Americans myriad possibilities but no real opportunities, and that the success of blaxploitation is at least partly due to the rise in black militant activism, a response to the same, near the beginning of the blaxploitation movement. I intend to give defense and justification to this much-maligned part of American culture, and to create a more enlightened discussion on race and film in America.

A STUDY OF THE WOMAN'S ROLE AND STAR PERSONAS IN THE FILMS OF FRANK CAPRA

Mackenzie R. Deese, (Dr. Susan Crutchfield), Department of English, UW-La Crosse 1725 State St. La Crosse, WI 54601

The Golden Era of cinema (1930–1950) produced some of the most memorable and influential films thoughout history. One of the most influential directors of this time was Frank Capra. In Capra's films audiences get a taste of hard-pressing traditional American values; however at the same time, Capra produced some of the most complex and progressive female characters during this time of female supression. This study explores Capra's use of female characters and their roles in his films as well as how the actresses' star personas affect the portrayal of the characters. More specifically, this research inquires how the star personas of actresses, Barbara Stanwyck and Jean Arthur, affect the female characters they portray in Capra's films and how the actresses' star personas affect how audiences respond to the characters as well as the films. Along with reading scholarly articles and books on the films and actors, research will be conducted in January 2010 at the UCLA film archives where the films will be viewed in their original format along with additional research which includes, but is not limited to, news reels of the films and actors, interviews with Capra, Stanwyck, and Arthur, director's notes, and audition tapes. The findings will be analyzed in order to make correlations among the films, the actresses' star personas, the female characters, and audience response. It is anticipated that Stanwyck and Arthur's star personas will have an effect on the type of female characters they portray in Capra's films as well as how the films were perceived by audiences.

THE (CINEMATIC) DARK KNIGHT: THE DEVELOPMENT OF BRUCE WAYNE, BATMAN AND THE CHARACTERS AROUND THEM

Author: Brian Fitzgerald Faculty Mentor: John Daly Department: History Institution: State University of New York College at Brockport 350 New Campus Drive Brockport, NY 14220

In the winter session of 2013 at the State University of New York College at Brockport, I attended a history class called "History on Film" with Professor Dr. John Daly. For the final in this class, Dr. Daly gave us the task of looking at any genre of films or groups of films and to create an argument around those films. Taking this opportunity to look at films in a scholarly setting, I tasked myself with looking at the character of Bruce Wayne aka Batman through the years. I wanted to see how the characters in the film compared to the original comic released in 1939. I also wanted to see if the films reflected more of the social issues that were relevant during the time of their release and the audience interest of that time. Over the seventy year history of Batman films, the characters of both the Batman, or Bruce Wayne, and the villainous Joker have been interpreted in very different and distinct ways. My study highlights how Batman films have reflected the cultural concerns of the era in which they were made in both the plot and characters. Each character was originally created by comic book artist Bob Kane in the late 1930's and developed further in the years after. The films started off as campy, fun filled adventures, beginning in the 1943 serial release and the 1966 Adam West feature. The films moved towards a darker tone in the 1989 Tim Burton films and finally into the realistic Nolan trilogy. As the films progressed through the century, the characters became closer interpretations of the original characters, reflecting the darker and intellectual side of each more clearly. Each film also portrayed different cultural issues of the films' release, including the fear of a Japanese invasion of the 1940's and the tension of the Cold War during the 1960's.

Conclusion

Most film degree programs in the predominantly English-speaking countries require two to three semesters of film history, covering mainly Eurocentric cinema history. Hence, the need to broaden the curriculum to incorporate non-Western film accounts. The possibilities for topics to choose from in the category of film history are virtually limitless. The history of Native American film practices, for example, would be a good research topic. A biography of a little-known Native American filmmaker from the Blackfeet reservation in Montana would be an original contribution. That is what film history is, stories about people making the movies that bring something new into the world, one person at a time.

Questions for Discussion

- Does our historical perspective change over time?
- How is knowledge of film history created?
- How does knowledge of film history influence the filmmaking process?
- How has digital technology affected film production, distribution, and exhibition?

References

Furay, C., & Salevouris, M. J. (1988). *The methods and skills of history: A practical guide*, 2nd ed. Hoboken, NJ: John Wiley & Sons, Inc.

Santayana, G. (1906). *Life of reason: Reason in science*. New York: Charles Scribner's Sons.

von Schlegel, F. (1991). *Philosophical fragments*. Minneapolis, MIN: University of Minnesota Press.

12

INTEGRATING FILM THEORY WITH FILM PRODUCTION

> Teaching filmmaking without being cognizant of fundamental cinematic theories means film craft to the mere level of an amateur workshop. And the opposite: studying film history and theory without a corresponding experience in the elemental aspects of filmmaking leaves theoretical research without a solid basis, forcing students to plunge into abstraction.
>
> Lev Kuleshov

> The recent emergence of the audiovisual essay in the study of film presses the use of images further and generates experiments with the critical potential of evoking and directly engaging the very objects it examines. Images are used to study images; film becomes quotable in its criticism.
>
> Hoi Lun Law

> Having a really good understanding of history, literature, psychology, sciences —is very, very important to actually being able to make movies.
>
> George Lucas

Summary

Undergraduate students greatly benefit from reading film theory as it helps them think more deeply about their own movie productions. This chapter will outline some of the major film theory movements, discussing effective ways to incorporate them in the undergraduate curriculum. Within this context, the creative and critical potential of the audiovisual film essay, a novel format of critical analysis, will be examined. An extension of the written essay format itself, the audiovisual essay is a multimedia text that combines video, audio, and written elements to convey a thesis-driven argument, collapsing the distinction between film theoretical analysis and the process of film production. A variety of undergraduate audiovisual essays and informative websites on how to produce them are included for your perusal.

What Is Film Theory?

Film theory is the ability to speculate about general principles and properties of film. Whereas film history analyzes patterns of continuity and change in the way specific films are produced and viewed over time, film theory is a philosophical inquiry into the nature and functions of film in general. Film theorists tend, in fact, to ask abstract, broad questions about the medium of film:

- What is film? What is a film made out of that makes it a film rather than something else? Is a film made out of celluloid, light beams, photographs, editing, time, or feelings? (ontological questions)
- What is the proper use of film techniques? What makes a scene powerful or mediocre? What criteria underlie our values and evaluations? (aesthetic questions)
- What is the relation of film to society and politics, and to society's economic institutions? What is the relation of film to history? How has film been used and regarded? (ideological questions)
- How is a spectator able to comprehend a film? What makes meanings occur to the viewer? How are we able to think and know something through a film? (epistemological questions)

Learning how to answer these types of questions helps undergraduate students understand the ways in which movies produce and deliver meaning, thus improving their ability to make better-informed choices during film production.

Since the 1960s, influential and often contested theoretical paradigms such as semiotics, post-structuralism, neo-Marxism, psychoanalytic theory, feminism, cultural studies, postcolonial studies, and postmodernism have attempted to explain how films impact our worldviews, affecting our goals, relationships, and social interactions. By becoming more aware of how cinema influences human behavior and community life, undergraduate students end up producing socially conscious films with relevant content. For example, by using feminist film theories to analyze the representation of female characters in Alfred Hitchcock's films, undergraduate students can become aware of how cultural constructs of gender influence their sense of self and the way they relate to each other, learning how to develop round and dynamic characters in their scripts. Along the same vein, becoming acquainted with 1970s apparatus theory, derived in part from Marxist film theory, helps undergraduates understand how governmental organizations and institutions have utilized cinema as a powerful propaganda instrument.

Film Theory in the Undergraduate Curriculum

For most undergraduate students, film theory presents a great challenge; like mathematics or theoretical physics, just a minority of film majors seems predisposed to do well in it. Yet, no matter what predisposition a student has, studying film theory at the undergraduate level has been shown to greatly increase students' critical thinking skills. Unfortunately, the majority of bachelor film degree curricula require only a couple of classes in film theory (usually one class in classical and one in contemporary film theory), offering further film studies seminars that adopt a theoretical approach as electives (typically attended by undergraduate students with a penchant for theoretical analysis!). Hence, the importance of offering a wide range of film studies elective courses that utilize diverse theoretical frameworks to analyze popular films and trendy movie genres among undergraduates.

Film industry professionals, and oftentimes film production teachers, fail to recognize the fruitful link between film studies and movie production, dismissing the importance of study the art of filmmaking from a theoretical perspective; thus, the "bad rap" film studies courses tend to have among undergraduate students. Then, how can university professors entice students to read film theory?

First of all, film studies instructors can analyze the work of popular directors who have incorporated theoretical notions such as the "male gaze" (feminist film theory) or "ideological indoctrination" (Marxist film theory) into their pictures. By understanding the effective imbrication of theory and practice in the films of successful filmmakers, students realize that a critical understanding of film is essential to the realization of their own film projects. Quentin Tarantino's body of work offers a perfect case study that could attract many undergraduate students. Not only does his pastiche of film genres and styles provide the opportunity to review important contributions to the history of international cinema (e.g., the French New Wave, the Italian Spaghetti Western Movement, etc.), Tarantino's films deal with themes and characters that perfectly lend themselves to the discussion of sociopolitical issues such as racism and sexism through a theoretical lens. For example, film students could examine *Django Unchained* (2012), a film that tells the story of a former black slave who is on a quest to rescue his wife from the grips of a slave owner, in terms of racial stereotypes. Does Tarantino's revisionist historical film contribute to deconstructing racial assumptions about black men as being violent and threatening? Or rather, does it perpetuate the same longstanding stereotypes of black men as individuals to be feared? These kinds of questions help undergraduates better comprehend how theoretical concerns and concepts can make their film productions compelling and successful.

Alternatively, an undergraduate project in film theory can be conducted as part of a faculty research study. From working closely with film studies professors, undergraduate students learn to accomplish tasks such as (1) performing a bibliographic search; (2) writing a literature review; (3) conducting surveys, questionnaires, and interviews; (4) analyzing film clips; and (5) evaluating research data. Mentoring students in faculty research is a win-win scenario as there are significant benefits for both sides: while undergraduates develop critical research skills that can be applied to their own creative and theoretical work, film studies professors can save considerable time and efforts that can be utilized for assessing and cross-referencing research findings.

Another way to ease undergraduates into studying film theory is through independent studies with a faculty whose expertise lies in theoretical methodologies for the study of cinema. In order to be original, an independent studies project in film theory might examine a local filmmaker's body of work that has never been analyzed by a third party; utilize qualitative methods for the assessment of high school students' experience and usage of film editing software such as Adobe Premiere or Final Cut Pro; or analyze the ways in which digital technology has influenced patterns of movie exhibition and moviegoing in a small town. Additional suggestions follow.

Possible Topics for Research in Film Theory

- Study cognitive dissonance in the storytelling style and aesthetic approach of specific filmmakers.
- Analyze the subjective nature of documentary representation through the lens of film semiotics.
- Research why some undergraduate film majors dislike studying theory.
- Investigate effects of early education in film theory, at different levels.
- Analyze the body of work of a local filmmaker about whom there are not available studies.
- Connect film theory with other studies such as computer science, psychology, or mathematics.
- Investigate some of the ways in which film theory informs film production.
- Do qualitative research on why some film production professors do not teach any film theory. Ask for tips from the ones who do.
- Explore ways that interactive web documentaries can be analyzed.
- Collect and summarize resources for teaching film theory as part of film production instruction.
- Compare film theory classes offered at different universities (theories studied, required film theory courses, types of assignments, etc.).
- Experiment with a peer-mentoring program for film theory.
- Do a meta-analysis of google reviews of film theory textbooks.
- Interview film theory professors to document and analyze the effectiveness of various pedagogical tools.

- Analyze the ideological effects of specific film genres, and compare and contrast them.
- Discuss the cinematic representation of minority ethnic groups through the lens of postcolonial theory.
- Analyze the audiovisual historical construction of national identity.
- Investigate the ways in which postmodern documentary films tend to blur the boundaries between fiction and nonfiction.
- Discuss documentary filmmaking as social justice activism.

Bridging the Gap between Film Theory and Film Production: The Audiovisual Essay

The digital age gave rise to a new format of film analysis: the audiovisual essay. An extension of the written essay format, the audiovisual essay mixes audio, video, and text files into the same digital platform to convey a thesis-driven argument. During the past decade, the audiovisual essay has received accolades from all over the world, encouraging film scholars and film reviewers alike to creatively edit images, video clips, and sounds in their critical analyses of films. Academic institutions around the globe have increasingly begun to incorporate audiovisual essay assignments in their film courses and online film journals are adopting audiovisual criticism more and more, overcoming the limitations of the frame-by-frame analysis.

Over the last two decades, the availability of DVD extras and the development of nonlinear editing software have been instrumental in expanding film studies scholars' analytical toolbox and techniques. By looking at the bonus material packed on a disk and by having the opportunity to recombine film clips with images, sound bites, and textual commentaries, film scholars and film students alike have produced new kinds of critical understandings of cinema that collapse the boundaries between makers and critics. In adopting audiovisual means to analyze films, not only do they circumvent convoluted passages in writing to describe a scene or sequence, they also avoid mediating a sensorial experience into words proving films' ability to evoke feelings and emotions. And although the audiovisual essay has raised questions about academic rigor and integrity—some film studies scholars have resisted adopting the audiovisual format considering it the realm of the amateur cinephile—the audiovisual essay seems to appeal to those undergraduate students for whom the study of film theory presents a great challenge.

Samples Abstracts Submitted to NCUR

www.cur.org/what/events/students/ncur/past/abstracts/

THE HITCHCOCK BLONDE AND HOW SHE DRIVES THE THRILLER

Donnie B. Lambert, (Dr. Elizabeth Heffelfinger), English/Film Department, Western Carolina University Cullowhee NC, 28723.

The Hitchcock Blonde and How She Drives the Thriller. Alfred Hitchcock is known for his stylish films that explore themes such as sex, crime, and murder. He is also known for the "Hitchcock Blonde": an icy, mysterious blonde woman that proves to be an important element in the structure of his important films, including *Vertigo* (1958) and *The Birds* (1963). The Hitchcock Blonde's motives are typically concealed from other characters in the narrative but laid out for the audience to see; thus, she is a character of deception and mystery. While many critical analyses argue the function and purpose of the Hitchcock Blonde in Hitchcock films, I will show that the she is more than just an iconic character. She is also responsible for the downfall and ultimate demise of the protagonist. In order to accomplish this feat, the Hitchcock Blonde hides her true intentions from the protagonist, she highlights the flaws of the protagonist through her sexual implications, and she perpetuates the narrative by being directly related to the antagonizing force of the film which is working against the male protagonist. I also show that her function is to work against the protagonist is such a way that she can be considered the villain of the film. These elements of the Hitchcock Blonde can be seen throughout the catalog of the director's films but is most prevalent in the four films between 1958 and 1962: *Vertigo, North by Northwest* (1959), *Psycho* (1960), and *The Birds* (respectively). These films mark the peak of Alfred Hitchcock's film career; they have turned such stars as Tippi Hedren and Eva Marie Saint into Hitchcock Blondes, women who influence whether we as an audience view the protagonist as a hero, a failure, or a villain.

STEREOTYPICAL REPRESENTATIONS OF AFRICA IN *THE GHOST AND THE DARKNESS*

Tyler T. Auffhammer (Dr. Elizabeth Heffelfinger) English Department, Western Carolina University, Cullowhee, NC 28723

Stephen Hopkins' 1996 film, *The Ghost and the Darkness*, is a fictionalized account of the Tsavo Man-Eaters, notorious man-eating lions that were responsible for the deaths of numerous construction workers on the Kenya-Uganda Railway in 1898. This paper explores how the film's setting and historical reference, a period of British colonialism in Africa, reinvigorates conventional African myths and is the catalyst for stereotypical representations of Africa. The first representation of Africa depicts it as a large reservoir of resources available for the taking by Westerners. This is presented through the colonial exploitation of Africa by means of the construction of the Kenya-Uganda Railway. By displaying the rise in colonial exploitation in Africa near the turn of the 19th century and the use of African workers to exploit themselves, harkening back to the myth of the submissive African slave, the setting of the film is the catalyst for the representation of Africa as a land of resources to be acquired by Western nations. The second representation of Africa promotes the idea that Africa is a helpless land that needs the power of Western nations to protect it. Africans are rendered as feeble and incompetent while the popular myth of strong Westerners with big guns and safari hats is embodied. Thus, the film's setting fosters the representation of Africa as dependent on the protection of Western nations. The third representation of Africa fostered in the film illustrates Africa as a savage land that must be conquered by the Westerners. The man-eating lions are shown to be vicious and elusive, the latter trait leading to the Africans dubbing them "the Ghost and the Darkness." Only with the skills, technology, and natural willpower of the Westerners are the lions defeated. Through the exploration of the stereotypical representations of Africa depicted in *The Ghost and the Darkness*, we obtain a better understanding of the consistent circulation, even in more recent films, of these colonial era tropes.

LIGHTS, CAMERA, CULTURE: EXPLORING AMERICANS' PERCEPTION OF FRENCH CINEMA

Caitlin Cleveland, Aurélie Van de Wiele, Department of Modern Languages and Intercultural Studies, Salisbury University, 1101 Camden Ave. Salisbury, MD, 21801

Pop music, movies, T.V. series … countless elements of American popular culture are appreciated around the world. On the other end, mainstream America seems more reluctant to embrace foreign popular cultures. Cinema is a salient example of this trend. By looking at the highest grossing films in two of the top five feature film producing countries, France and the United States, one can observe the obvious disconnect between the United States and other nations regarding film importations. In this study, I will aim to unveil the reasons behind Americans' lack of interest in foreign cinema by examining French films. I will do so by exploring the concept of "culture" itself and the impact it has on one's tastes. Perceptions are influenced by one's own culture, which anthropologist Edward Hall defines as "a highly selective screen between man and the outside world. It designates what we pay attention to and what we ignore." As perceptions and tastes are shaped by culture, individuals often find themselves unable to relate to cultural elements that are foreign, and ultimately choose to reject them. This dynamic, I argue, is at the center of Americans' lack of attraction for French cinema. I claim that certain cultural differences between France and the United States explain Americans' reluctance to embrace French cinema. More particularly, my study demonstrates that anthropological, psychological, and historical contrasts, which influence the two countries' perceptions of the role of cinema in society, the definitions of humor and of a successful movie, are at stake here. This research will reach far beyond what we see at the movies. By focusing on the root of cultural differences and perceptions, we can begin to understand the differences in perceptions on a larger scale, such as religion, economics, or politics.

SUBHUMAN-REPRESENTING WOMEN IN FILM

Mikayla Daniels, Mentor Elisha Miranda, Department of Film, Eastern Washington University,526 5th St, Cheney, WA 99004

SUBHuman is a sci-fi action script set in a dystopian world where the rich reign and those born imperfect are enslaved. Fiona is a SUB (Scientifically Undesirable Bio form) who is raised without knowledge of her humanity and treated as property. When a traumatic event brings Fiona to a place where she meets her perfect sister, the women come together to stop the forces that are oppressing the SUB's. This script speaks to many social issues such as: class separation, patriarchal society, fertility and gender issues. The intent of this script is to not only tell a great story that will hopefully inspire discussion but also to create characters that are largely underrepresented in the Hollywood majority. My Hero is not only a woman but one born with a physical disability. It's Fiona's missing left arm that casts her into the enslaved class and yet she is ultimately the one who holds the power. A report by San Diego State University film professor Martha Lauzen states that "the top 100 grossing films of 2013 were overwhelmingly male. Just 15% of protagonists, 29% of major characters and 30% of all speaking characters were female."(Saba) I propose to exhibit a staged reading of several key scenes from my script that will be performed by some of the Spokane area's local acting talent. By presenting this reading I hope to positively represent women in film, as both a writer and, director. Few women are represented on screen in scripts with a feminist forward thinking analysis, even fewer are produced screenwriters and directors of the content created. There is a severe shortage of women in the industry: "Out of 1,452 filmmakers, 20.5% were women, but just 7% were directors. 19.5% of the writers were women, as were 22.7% of the producers" (Forbes). Forbes. "Geena Davis Institute New Research Shows That Girls and Women Are Missing Onscreen and Behind the Scenes Worldwide." *Forbes Magazine*. Web. 28 Nov. 2014. . Saba Hamedy "Report: Just 15% of Lead Characters in Major Movies Are Female." *Los Angeles Times. Los Angeles Times*, 11 Mar. 2014. Web. 24 Nov. 2014.

MASCULINITY AND ITS COUNTERTYPE IN PRE-NAZI GERMANY: READING VOLKER SCHLÖNDORFF'S *DER JUNGE TÖRLESS* (1966) THROUGH GEORGE L. MOSSE'S *THE IMAGE OF MAN*

Christopher P. Graves, (Dr. Hans-Bernhard Moeller), Department of Germanic Studies, University of Texas at Austin, Austin, TX 78712

In *Der junge Törless* (1966), first-time director Volker Schlöndorff provided what was lacking in West German film up to that date: an incisive historical and psychological examination of the causes of National Socialism. Set in an Austrian military academy during the fin de siècle, the film focuses on Törless, a withdrawn, reflective cadet, as he struggles over his involvement in the secret, sadistic torturing of another classmate, Basini, by two of his friends, Beineberg and Reiting. Although there is widespread agreement among film scholars that Schlöndorff's *Der junge Törless* is a parable of Nazi Germany, little to no attention is paid to a close examination of the socio-psychological dynamics at work between the students that are productive of National Socialism. Utilizing George L. Mosse's *The Image of Man*, an historical treatment of the solidification of modern masculinity in Western Europe, this essay argues that central to the fascist dynamics at work between Törless, Basini, Beineberg, and Reiting is an uncompromising masculinity that codifies through violence a binary between the masculine type and its countertype. After situating this dynamic in its presupposition—the failure of institutions such as the academy to understand, incorporate, and work through such aggressiveness—I chart how both Törless and Basini, as countertypes, are compelled to perform masculinity given the threat of bodily violence posed to them by Beineberg and Reiting, both as representative of the newly developing fascist man. Drawing on Mosse's conceptualization of the *Männerbund* to explain the subsequent expulsion of Basini from the community of men, I argue that the sexual and bodily violence perpetrated against Basini serves to consolidate the masculine heterosexuality of both Beineberg and Reiting. Although Törless is implicated as an ambivalent spectator to Basini's torture, I explore how his lived, embodied engagement with Basini apart from Beineberg and Reiting serves as the material presupposition to an ethical maturity which rejects fascist masculinity. Despite the fact that I concede that at the film's closing Törless still partly evidences a lack of understanding regarding masculinity, I assert that what is of value in *Der junge Törless* is the example Schlöndorff provides of Törless's embodiedness: this conception does justice to the bodily dimension of the internalization of the norms and values of fascism and the method of critiquing such values through an embodied engagement with a countertype that illuminates one's larger social responsibilities.

Samples of Audiovisual Essays

Film Seminar, 381: *QUENTIN TARANTINO & THE CINEMA OF COOL.* Professor Lucia Ricciardelli, School of Film & Photography, Montana State University (Fall 2018)

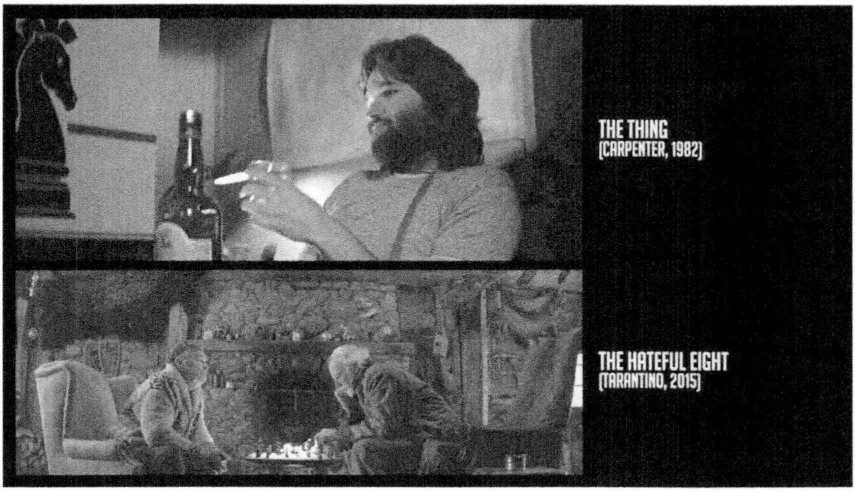

FIGURE 12.1 A Hateful Love Letter to The Thing. Arlen Guest, Mentor Lucia Ricciardelli.

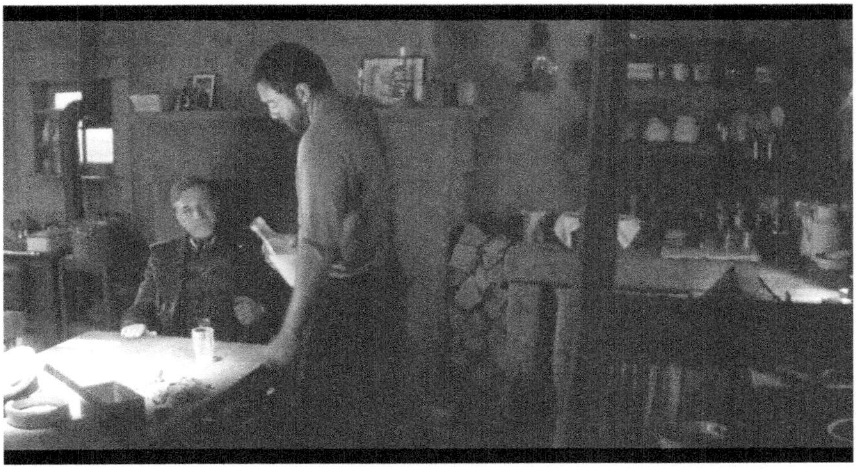

FIGURE 12.2 Tarantino's Most Chilling and Terrifying Movie Villain: Colonel Landa. Noah Correia, Mentor Lucia Ricciardelli.

Conclusion

Though many undergraduate students struggle to understand the relevance of reading film theory, it is undeniable that its study pervades their film productions in more ways than they realize. Becoming aware of how popular films have been informed by theoretical discussions of contemporary sociopolitical

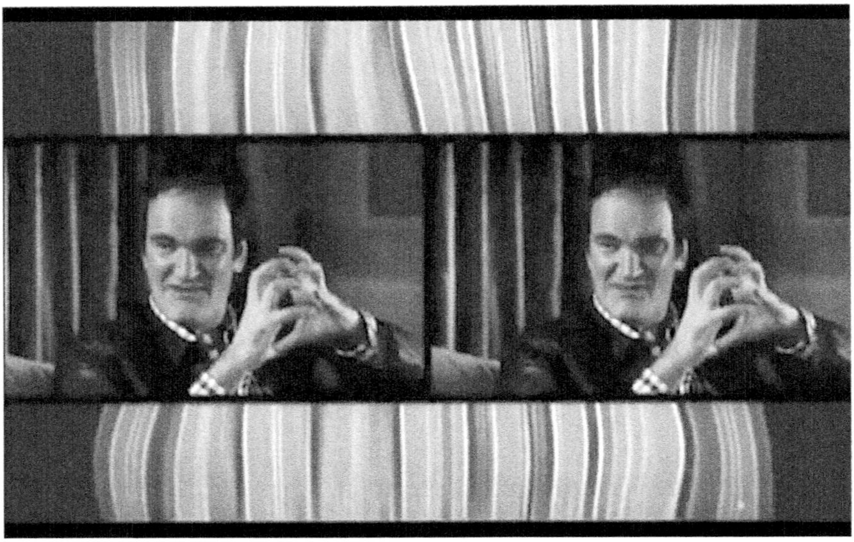

FIGURE 12.3 Quentin Tarantino & Music. Tapweski Sandaine, Mentor Lucia Ricciardelli.

issues helps students realize that theory is not as irrelevant to filmmaking success as people working in the film industry might argue. Additionally, careful attention to the relationship between theory and practice in the film undergraduate curriculum helps establish academic rigor, lending credibility to the discipline of film within the university circuit.

Questions for Discussion

- What is the relative importance of film theory with respect to film production and why?
- How does the study of film theory influence the process of making a film?
- How does original research relate to your previous courses?
- How can you make your project applicable to your future?
- How can you make an original contribution to the discipline of film theory?

References

Kuleshov, Lev (via Frank P. Tomasulo). Theory to Practice: Integrating Cinema Theory and Film Production. Cinema Journal Vol. 36, No. 3 (Spring, 1997), pp. 113–117.

Law, Hoi Lun on ANGST/FEAR (Adrian Martin & Cristina Álvarez López, 2014) Available at: http://reframe.sussex.ac.uk/audiovisualessay/reflections/reflections-on-av-essays/hoi-lun-law-on-angstfear-adrian-martin-cristina-alvarez-lopez-2014/

Lucas, George. What It Takes (Podcast). October 27, 2017. Available at: https://learningenglish.voanews.com/a/what-it-takes-george-lucas/4082398.html

13

FILM EDUCATION IN THE INFORMATION AGE

> With the growing popularity in e-learning, it occurred to me that the e should mean more than electronic. If we are going to call it e-learning, shouldn't it be effective, efficient, and engaging?
>
> M. David Merrill

> Education is the most powerful weapon which you can use to change the world.
>
> Nelson Mandela

> When you learn, teach. When you get, give.
>
> Maya Angelou

> Students do not learn much just sitting in classes listening to teachers, memorizing prepackaged assignments, and spitting out answers. They must talk about what they are learning, write reflectively about it, relate it to past experiences, and apply it to their daily lives. They must make what they learn part of themselves.
>
> Arthur W. Chickering and Stephen C. Ehrmann

Summary

Visuals aids can have a huge impact on how we process and retain information as images are easier to recall than words and abstract concepts, and thus can be utilized to facilitate student learning at the undergraduate level. This chapter lays out pedagogical tools to help foster undergraduate instruction, focusing on the effective use of visual aids, computer technology, and the internet as powerful means to perform research and increase knowledge retention. This discussion is followed by an overview of relevant topics in film education from both a disciplinary and interdisciplinary perspective.

Introduction

Only three decades have passed since Tim Berners-Lee invented the World Wide Web and our lives have been transformed in countless ways. The use of digital technology has become a large portion of our everyday life and the way we operate, especially with regard to millennials. We rely on smartphones, tablets, computers, and various types of software to solve problems, perform financial and bureaucratic transactions, as well as for entertainment. We tend to communicate with each other more and more through emojis, memes, and GIFs, purchase visual rendering of commodities, and advertise our personas via selfies routinely posted on our social media profiles. While print culture is certainly not going to disappear, we can safely say that in the 21st century, Western culture has become predominantly visual. In particular, the millennial generation, which has not witnessed such a radical cultural transformation, seems to mainly operate visually. Needless to say, colleges and universities have had to change their pedagogical tools in order to accommodate the visual learner's needs.

How Can Digital Technology Support Teaching and Facilitate Learning?

Digital technology and the World Wide Web have had a huge impact on the ways in which students and teachers approach knowledge. Not only has the internet made it easier and quicker to find information, it has also allowed us to become "experts" in many fields by just browsing through a variety of do-it-yourself videos that range from projects for beginners to more complex and intricate tasks. Yet, due to the vast amount of unverifiable data on the World Wide Web, it has become increasingly important to distinguish between reliable and unreliable information (Prelinger, 2007). So, how can teachers and students alike utilize the power of digital technology to support teaching and facilitate learning? What are the benefits of the internet and computer technology in the classroom? What kinds of applications are available to help students learn film production skills? Are film education curricula at the university level changing to reflect this new state of affairs?

Undergraduate students seem to learn best when knowledge is presented using audiovisual aids, especially with regard to theoretical concepts and complicated subjects. Audiovisual aids for learning can vary from infographics, photos, charts, and posters to PowerPoint presentations (or equivalents), video clips, films, and audiovisual essays. Delivering information in a visually creative way helps increase knowledge retention and contributes to students' enthusiasm about a topic, encouraging them to perform further research. Not only does the use of images, audio, and videos create a sensory experience that is more immersive, fostering student engagement with the material presented, it also facilitates remote learning opportunities through online courses. Because of this, it has become increasingly common for teachers to utilize laptops and tablets, and to let students use their own smartphones to download applications to help their learning in the classroom and at home.

Additionally, the ready availability of computer technology and the internet has made archives more accessible to students, boosting their interest in archival research. Before the World Wide Web became publicly available, the archive was in fact mainly the realm of professional historians and academic researchers. From Google Scholar and university library databases to private and public archives, the internet provides access to a vast array of primary and secondary sources that students can browse from everywhere at any time. A prime example of online data collection is *The September 11 Digital Archive* (2002–2018), which "uses electronic media to collect, preserve, and present the history of September 11, 2001 and its aftermath" (Figure 13.1). In addition to easing the process of research, this type of online project can be used to encourage undergraduate students to develop their own digital archive and reflect upon its construction: What records did you select? What data did you discard and why? What are the principles that govern your filing system's logic? Class activities such as these contribute to developing and refining students' research abilities and critical skills.

Undergraduate film projects can also utilize the internet to implement quantitative and qualitative research methods by having students collect data through online surveys, questionnaires, and interviews. To carry out his research project on YouTube restricting and demonetizing LGBTQ videos, for example, BFA student Thomas Callahan conducted a series of online surveys and questionnaires,

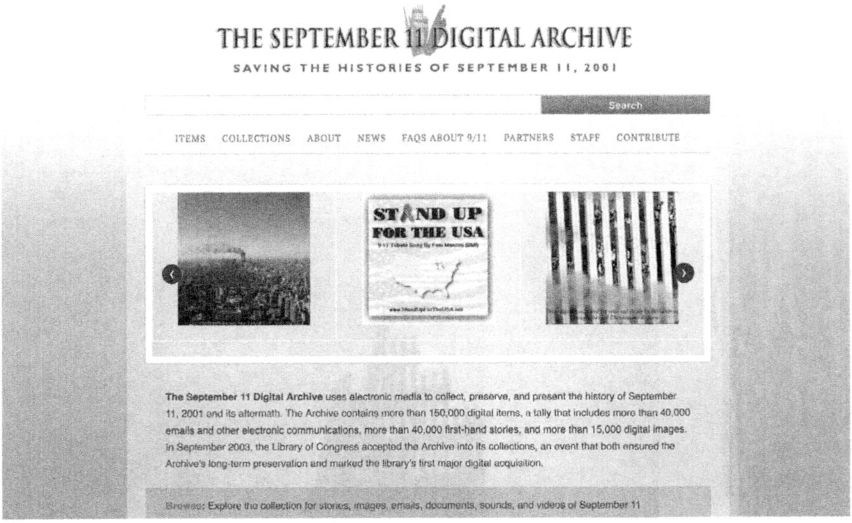

FIGURE 13.1 *The September 11 Digital Archive http://911digitalarchive.org/*

asking undergraduate students attending MSU-Bozeman whether they agree or disagree with YouTube's censoring practices (Figure 13.2). Thomas first posted his survey questions on the School of Film & Photography's (MSU) Facebook page, then he sent them to other MSU departments' student email lists. Currently, he is planning to disseminate the surveys to other colleges and universities across the country using available student email lists and social media platforms.

Research in Film Education

Because the digital revolution is a fairly recent phenomenon, projects on the use of electronic audiovisual media as pedagogical tools can easily be the subject of original research. Film students are especially qualified to perform research in this area of education since audiovisual language learning is a crucial aspect of their undergraduate education. For example, film undergraduates could perform a study to assess the effectiveness of video tutorials on academic learning, or help record interview sessions for research projects conducted by students in other academic fields and then reflect on the benefit of such interdisciplinary collaboration. The possibilities for research in the field of film education are virtually limitless.

Recently the Council on Undergraduate Research (CUR) started a new division for Education. Surprisingly, most disciplinary areas were already represented, and it begs the question, "Why is education, a field that could serve as an umbrella for all undergraduate teaching, be one of the last divisions within CUR?" The answer lies mainly in the fact that departments of education focus primarily on preparing future teachers, and their curricula are so full of requirements from accreditation and public instruction mandates, that they did not think they had room for an undergraduate research requirement. However, when one takes a close look at what instructors study, what projects they

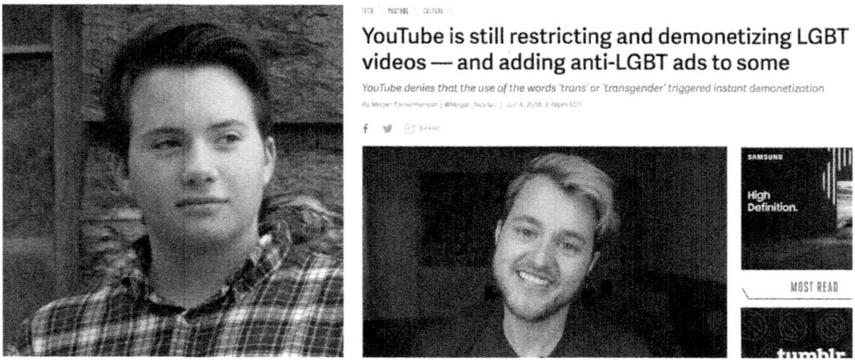

FIGURE 13.2 *Thomas Callahan's YouTube LGBTQ Discrimination Audiovisual Essay (fall 2018)* https://vimeo.com/311777295.

have to complete, and the importance of them passing on the magic of discovery to their future students, it made perfect sense to start this new CUR division. Another factor in this equation is that faculty have the ability to alter the curriculum slightly and make research part of the standard curriculum for education majors if they so choose.

Possible Topics in Film Education

Some possible research topics for projects in film education are:

- Design a curriculum for cinema therapy.
- Explore what kinds of teaching web-enabled technologies such as iPads and smartphones support, and whether they help achieve meaningful learning.
- Study the feasibility of film training classes through live video.
- Investigate what teaching tools can be used to keep students motivated and engaged while learning film theory.
- Conduct focus groups with film alumni who are teaching and have had undergraduate research experience to find out how it has been informing their teaching philosophy and approaches.
- Survey fellow film majors about perceptions of film education.
- Examine the role of mindfulness in classroom management.
- Assess the effectiveness of video tutorials on academic learning.
- Explore different learning styles to teach film.
    - Visual (spatial);
    - aural (auditory-musical);
    - verbal (linguistic);
    - physical (kinesthetic);
    - logical (mathematical);
    - social (interpersonal);
    - solitary (intrapersonal).

Possible Interdisciplinary Topics Related to Film Education

We can broaden the topic of film education research by evaluating its interdisciplinary potential with a variety of other fields. Here are a few examples:

- Film education and language learning methods.
- Film education and social and emotional development.
- Film education and oral history.
- Film education and environmental education.
- Film education and brain development.

- Film education and STEAM research.
- Film education and the dyslexic student.
- Film education and literary analysis.
- Film education and professional training.
- Film education and indigenous research methodologies.
- Film education across cultural boundaries.

Conclusion

Over the past three decades, rapid advancements in digital and information technologies, together with the increased widespread availability and affordability of computer equipment and internet access, have significantly impacted teaching methods and students' learning. The benefits of utilizing digital means such as PowerPoint, audiovisual essays, iPads and smartphones, multimedia platforms, and social media as pedagogical tools are undisputable. Not only have they helped increase students' retention of information and enhanced their proficiency in archival research, they have also allowed for distance learning and contributed to improving undergraduates' digital literacy and critical thinking skills. Film students are especially qualified to perform research in education at this historical juncture due to their mastery of audiovisual language and predisposition to being audiovisual learners and communicators.

Questions for Discussion

- Why is research in film education needed?
- How does film education research reach film teachers?
- Why is ongoing research important for film educators?
- Can we transfer these discovery ideas to students in K-12 classrooms?

References

Angelou, M. (2011). *Oprah's master class* [Interview]. Retrieved from www.oprah.com/app/master-class.html.

Chickering, A. W., & Ehrmann, S. C. (1996). Implementing the seven principles: Technology as lever. *AAHE Bulletin*. Retrieved from www.researchgate.net/publication/246430027_Implementing_the_Seven_Principles_Technology_as_Lever.

Mandela, N. (June 23, 1990). Speech at Madison Park High School. Boston, MA.

Merrill, M. D. (2012). *First principles of instruction*. Hoboken, NJ: Pfeiffer.

Prelinger, R. (2007). Archives and access in the 21st century. *Cinema Journal*, *46*(3). Retrieved from https://is.muni.cz/el/1421/podzim2007/FAVK007/um/cinema_journal_02.pdf.

The September 11 Digital Archive (2002–2018). Center for History and New Media and American Social History Project/Center for Media and Learning. Retrieved from http://911digitalarchive.org/.

14

FILM TECHNOLOGY IN THE DIGITAL AGE

> We are in an electronic technology age now and it's about time we put away the old stuff.
>
> Monica Edwards

> A growing sub-genre of documentary film, the animated documentary poses a network of challenging, existential questions for the form. And while purists might cling to traditional, sanctioned mores, a healthy re-evaluation of our inventory is inspiring filmmakers to experiment and push the boundaries.
>
> Beige Luciano-Adams

> It is as if all of us have set out on a virtual journey to a new country—call it Digital Land—where we must learn new customs and a new language.
>
> Timothy Gunn

Summary

The birth and history of film are partially premised on the invention of a series of technological devices—the camera, the printer, the Moviola, and the projector—and their subsequent advances. Although cinema is also the outcome of sociopolitical demands and economic interests, the notion of technological progress has always been a crucial factor in its development. A variety of topic areas will be examined in this chapter, including the passage from analog to digital technology and its impact on the film production process, and the interactive storytelling format. Sample projects and abstracts will show students some possibilities for film technological research, followed by questions for discussion.

Introduction

Only a few decades have passed since it became possible to shoot a film digitally and digital technology has already turned out to be the preferred way to produce movies. Analogue movie cameras, film reels, and chemical printing have become obsolete in the contemporary electronic world, with digital cameras supplanting mechanical ones, computers and software taking the place of optical printers, and flashcards and external hard drives replacing film canisters. The implications of the shift from analogue to digital have been numerous, from making the filmmaking process more efficient, safer, and less expensive to creating the conditions for the emergence of interactive storytelling and computer-animated documentary, a subcategory of computer animation.

Currently, all the stages of film production, from writing a script and creating a preliminary budget to shooting, editing, and distributing a film, are almost entirely accomplished digitally. Most film theaters around the globe have converted their screens from film to digital, and half of those screens have been outfitted with 3-D projectors. Additionally, the internet has made it possible for filmmakers, whether professionals or amateurs, to showcase their film online through digital platforms such as YouTube or Vimeo, reaching a broader international audience and cutting down significantly the costs for film distribution and exhibition. But how exactly has the passage from analog to digital technology impacted the process of film production for both professional filmmakers and film students?

The Impact of Digital Technology on the Filmmaking Process

Although a few big budget films are still shot using 35mm and 70mm film cameras, the global film industry is presently relying mostly on digital equipment. Over the past decade, only a small percentage of Hollywood movies have been shot using analog cameras; Quentin Tarantino, Christopher Nolan, and Wes Anderson are among the few mainstream filmmakers who still prefer, and can afford, shooting on film. Some of the main reasons why digital cameras have become the industry standard is that they allow cinematographers to film at higher resolution and also lowered the production costs. The prices of digital equipment keep decreasing and now seem to be within the reach of the average person, permitting everybody with a DSLR camera (or even with just a smartphone or iPad), a computer, and editing software (editing applications such as QuickTime or iMovie are free of charge) the opportunity to experiment with creating a movie. Needless to say, aspiring filmmakers and film students have been benefiting greatly from this state of affairs.

Footage shot digitally is also easier to edit. Editing software such as Adobe Premiere Pro, Final Cut Pro X, or Avid Media Composer offer easy project organization and faster access to footage and special effects. In the pre-digital age, in fact, filmmakers had to rely on manual techniques either during the shooting stage or in postproduction to create visual effects, making the process of adding the effects demanding and time-consuming. Digital technology has made this process simpler, quicker, and more effective, allowing editors to create stunning special effects that appear more realistic than the ones obtained with analog means.

Additionally, digitally recorded sound is higher in quality than analog-recorded audio, doesn't deteriorate, and can be stored on hard drives as digital files. The rise of laptops and applications such as Apple's GarageBand and Avid's Pro Tools and the availability of inexpensive digital mixers have allowed film students to produce multitrack recording at home with a PC and/or to collaborate with composers in different parts of the world sharing their creations online. Professional digital audio recorders and microphones are considerably more affordable, allowing film students to produce high-quality audio and sound effects for their productions (Beacham, 2017). Because of the affordability and ready availability of audio recording and mixing equipment, film students can develop skills in music composition, recording, sound synthesis, and sound design for film scoring. Working alongside music faculty and students, film majors can learn how to compose original music and collaborate on artistic works and projects. This combination of academic study, creative work, community involvement, and hands-on training produces well-rounded filmmakers and digital media artists.

As Tarantino's *Inglourious Basterds* (2009) showed us, film reels are extremely flammable (do you remember how Shoshanna set her movie theater on fire?), and tend to get damaged over time. The rapid transformation in data storage which came along with the advent of digital technology has made the process of preserving, storing, and handling a movie much safer, more cost effective, and almost effortless. Currently, professional filmmakers and film students alike use online servers and hard disks to store their movies, saving multiple files of the same film to avoid unpleasant consequences. And, of course, digital files take much less storage space than film reels.

Interactive Storytelling and Computer Animation

By presenting information through hypertext, a computer-based system that allows users to establish different paths through a corpus of related material, digital technology has given rise to a new form of film narrative structure: nonlinear, interactive storytelling. This new storytelling form offers computer users the option to navigate a film story through an intuitive menu and hyperlinks, and to choose their own narrative paths around the film's main subject, providing an alternative to the traditional three-part act structure used in mainstream filmmaking (Landow, 2006). This possibility of choosing the film's organizing principle through the electronic hypertext contributes to collapsing the clear-cut difference between production and consumption, giving undergraduate students more agency to interpret the story, thus encouraging them to reflect critically on the way movies shape meaning.

Another interesting outcome of digital technology is the computer-animated documentary. By showing aspects of life that cannot be filmed in live action, such as the emotional and psychological dimension of human experience, computer-generated animated documentaries have challenged documentarians' reliance on the objectivity of the camera, broadening the epistemological potential of documentary films. As Beige Luciano-Adams (2009) claimed,

> A growing sub-genre of documentary film, the animated documentary poses a network of challenging, existential questions for the form. And while purists might cling to traditional, sanctioned mores, a healthy re-evaluation of our inventory is inspiring filmmakers to experiment and push the boundaries.

Undergraduate film students can choose from a vast array of animation software from Adobe Flash Player, Synfig Studio, Adobe Animate, and OpenToonz to Autodesk Softimage, iClone, Maya, Blender, and Animatron (some of which are available online at no cost,) to experiment with creating computer animations about the real.

Possible Topics on Film and Technology

- Analyze interactive storytelling in video games.
- Examine online film exhibition via YouTube and Vimeo.
- Investigate how mobile technology has affected documentary filmmaking.
- Examine how copyright laws apply to new technologies and content.
- From eye to ear: the connections between film and music.
- Explore how digital technologies and the internet have democratized film production.
- Discuss the use of mobile technology in the production and postproduction stages of filmmaking.
- Reflect on you own creation of an interactive film story.
- Investigate film reception in the digital age: from the movie theater screen to the mobile screen.
- Compose your own film soundtrack using GarageBand and reflect on this creative practice.
- Discuss how computer technology has blurred the boundaries between production and consumption.
- Research and/or produce short animations sample libraries.

Sample Abstracts Submitted to NCUR

www.cur.org/conferences_and_events/student_events/ncur/archive/

THE WAY OF THE FUTURE: INFORMATION AGE IDENTITIES IN CONTEMPORARY CINEMA

Niles J. Schwartz (Michael Reynolds), Department of English, Hamline University, 1536 Hewitt Avenue, Saint Paul, MN 55104–1284.

This paper evaluates a new discourse current in mainstream cinema. Saturated in information, the new millennium has presented the symptoms of a new condition, wherein human beings are governed by vast cybernetic networks: a virtual landscape where organic behavior is simulated with technological "efficiencies" bent on creating a homogenous environment, quashing inconsistencies and idiosyncrasies. Yet as thought processes are estranged from multi-dimensional introspection, "identity" becomes confused, as the human subject loses a sense of historical lineage and concrete spacial relation in lieu of identifying solely with the time-and-space condensing demands of the society —a process that has devastating effects on interpersonal communication and morality. Mainstream filmmakers are now exploring this socio-moral quandary. The films of directors Michael Mann, Martin Scorsese, and Paul Greengrass, among others, are less exhibitions of their respective genres (be it action/noir, biopic, period, etc) as they are atmospheric exhortations of the post-human condition in a technological landscape, where information systems have quickened to the extent that life must be processed mechanically rather than developed organically. The heroes in these motion pictures struggle with their longing for "genuine" experience as compromised in the mechanics of a world where individuation is only possible as "simulation" within the fragile networks of mass communication and transportation that form society's controlling structures. The films are conspicuous given their motifs of cell phones, media, and hyperreal environments such as airports, hotels, and hospitals, yet period films by the same directors also show an immediate interest in constructs of control. Drawing on theories of cybernetics, videoscopy, the "post-human," and close readings of specific films, the paper aims to reveal how filmmakers are increasingly reflective of our new "post-globalization" world, addressing the issue of human identity's dissonance with structures of governance.

MARIA TODAY: THE ENDURING IMAGE OF METROPOLIS

Cameron Robinson. (Bonnie Orzolek) Art Foundation. Virginia Commonwealth University. 609 Bowe Street. Richmond, VA 23284–3047

Fritz Lang's femme fatale poises gracefully as a marker of the ages, a veritable spokeswoman for the new technological age, despite her octogenarian status. At the dawn of the film's official re-discovery, Lang's dystopian epic merits a modern re-examination. Unlike the rest of Lang's largely realized caveat, the robot Maria, called Futura, remains unattainable and as frightening as ever, a testament to the frightening ideals of humanoid robotics that haunt us still. Lang's villain may be even better accentuated with the newly found footage of Hel. Yet, even without the visual weight of Hel or her representation of misguided sexual tension, Futura made a lasting foundation for the following decades of robot based design, both in science fiction and reality. Her assumption of Maria's features solidified the fears Cabek first put forward in R. U. R. Her stoic metal face, maniacal laughter and emotionless grin, both in metal and assumed human form set the stage for whole of science fiction that followed. The robot Maria seems as modern today as she did in 1928, because she represents the last remnants of Lang's prediction that have not been wholly assumed by our modern world. The overwhelming architecture, man eating manufacturing machines, and diabolical capitalism already saturate the metropolises of today. We live in the once grand sets Lang fashioned from cardboard, ruled by theoretical Frederson's and CEO fat cats, slaves to an economy based on mass production. However, Maria is still an image, unrealized. She represents a realm of science fiction not yet integrated into society, and thus remains a figure of modernity; petrifying, powerful, and beautiful.

Conclusion

Film undergraduates can research the ways in which digitization has impacted film technology alongside their professors or on student-directed projects mentored by faculty members in film, art, music, and computer science. As discussed above, film technology is a field that holds rich potential for a variety of undergraduate research projects, whether interdisciplinary or not. For the purposes of undergraduate research, it may be helpful to narrow the focus down to a few key aspects of film technology. Interactive storytelling, computer-generated documentary animation, and the relationship between analog and digital technologies in film production are fertile areas to explore. Digital filmmaking and the technology that surrounds it are a constantly changing landscape. The pace of change due to its association with computer applications is rapid.

Questions for Discussion

- How has film technology changed our perception of reality?
- Where will film technology be in the future?
- Has the widespread availability and affordability of digital cameras and computers democratized the production of films?

References

Beacham, F. (2017, June 13). How the 1990s changed recording and music production forever. Retrieved from www.thebroadcastbridge.com/content/entry/8815/in-the-1990s-audio-recording-changed-forever.

Gunn, T. (1996). The effects of new technologies on independent film and video artists. *Leonardo*, *29*(4): 320–321.

Landow, G. P. (2006). *Hypertext 3.0: Critical theory and new media in an era of globalization.* Baltimore, MD: The Johns Hopkins University Press.

Luciano-Adams, B. (2009). When docs get graphic: Animation meets actuality. *International Documentary Association*. Retrieved from www.documentary.org/content/when-docs-get-graphic-animation-meets-actuality.

15

FILM AS A THERAPEUTIC TOOL

Cinematherapy is the process or practice of therapists instructing their clients to watch film(s) that are relevant to issues of personal distress and dysfunction, and provide some sort of pathway toward advancing therapeutic gain.

Jeremy Clyman

While film and video has long been used within psychological practice, researchers and practitioners have only just begun to explore the benefits of film and video production as therapy.

Joshua L. Cohen, J. Lauren Johnson, and Penelope P. Orr

Many new works in film and video call upon memories of the senses.

Laura Marks

Making a digital story is an empowering and healing experience for youth, who spend four days learning movie-making and video editing software, writing and recording their own narrative, compiling and editing photographs, and choosing their own soundtrack.

Y.O.U.T.H. Training Project

The body is our sensation, our felt emotion. The body is our experience of ourselves, our temple in which the light of spirit burns. Unconscious worlds, numinous worlds, worlds with high order and worlds with no apparent order can become known within the body, because of the body.

Janet Adler

Summary

Cinematherapy has been a growing area of interest among psychologists, providing a context for new approaches to mental health as well as a variety of faculty and student research projects in film. This recent approach to therapy offers patients practical tools for handling stress, anxiety, and depression constructively and for building deeper and healthier social connections through watching films. Considering that cinema is perhaps the most popular contemporary form of mass entertainment, cinematherapy's healing potential should not be underestimated. This chapter discusses the use of film as a therapeutic tool and offers thoughts to inspire discussion. Even film students who are not doing projects in psychology can benefit from reading the case studies and project ideas outlined below. Indeed, to write compelling and believable characters, and effectively communicate with actors, film students need to deeply understand human behavior, as well as become aware of their own psychological world and emotional landscape.

Introduction

Psychological research on cinema investigates how watching a film influences the human mind by asking questions such as: How do people behave when they view a movie? What happens at the level of the eye, the ear and the brain when we watch a film? How do representations of women and men onscreen affect gender relations? What gives cinema its deep psychological and emotional significance, as well as its power to influence social behavior and heal physical and mental illness, across vastly different cultural contexts? Over the past century, numerous film theorists have attempted to answer these questions using various psychoanalytic theories from Freudian and Jungian to Lacanian, but only a few have discussed film as a therapeutic tool. Undergraduate students interested in researching this topic might want to take advantage of this lack of literature on the subject.

Most college students today, regardless of major, carry around with them a library of films and videos on their phones, tablets, and computers. Those who have decided on a film major and who have persisted all the way to capstone courses such as senior film project or undergraduate research, undoubtedly have strong feelings about what filmmaking means to them. Yet, they often do not take the time to reflect on or write down their deepest thoughts about the ways in which watching a film might have either positive or negative effects on them and their peers. And although many film majors end up enrolling in psychology courses to fulfill part of their core requirements, those classes usually do not focus on the psychology of film. That is why specific theories that examine the effects that film has on the spectator's psyche (e.g., feminist film theory, reception theories, postcolonial theory, etc.) should become the foundation for the entire film degree. If film students have a solid grasp on psychology, they will indeed have greater success as screenwriters, directors, and actors. Conveying the deep meanings inherent in cinematic expression as well as understanding how a film can alter behavior, are both salient topics for those who wish to teach in a way that will have lasting impact.

Cinematherapy

Although the use of film as a therapeutic tool can be traced back to post-World War II, when clips from experimental videos were shown to veterans suffering from PTSD to relax them, it was in the 1970s that the camera started to be widely adopted as a confessional tool for the empowerment of women, ethnic minorities, and lesbian and gay communities. The advent of portable video equipment in this period was in fact a catalyst for the surge in popularity of confessional videos. Yet, even though there is an increasing number of therapists who are utilizing film as a healing device, there is not yet much research literature on the theory and practice of cinematherapy. Cinematherapy is therefore a fertile field for film research.

Psychologists embracing cinematherapy as a healing practice argue that films can have therapeutic effects on the audience by providing an outlet for spectators to express their feelings, embrace their fears, and face emotional pain (Clyman, 2013; Wolz, 2005). But how does cinematherapy work exactly? Cinematherapists ask their patients to watch films that portray situations and emotional dynamics like the ones they are working on in real life and, then, analyze the films' main themes during the counseling session. By examining the effects that films' visuals, sounds, music, characters, and plots have on their patients' psyches, cinematherapists help them become aware of their own self-destructive behaviors. Such awareness is key to the patient's healing process, as by reflecting on his/her own psychological impasse and discussing possible ways to overcome it, the patient can experience emotional release and psychological healing.

Cinematherapists rely on the multisensory quality of film to help their patients remember things from their past, to let their patients' memories repressed out of the conscious mind come to the surface as triggered by a film's haptic visuality. The term "haptic visuality" refers to "a sense of physical touching or being touched engendered by an organization of the film image in which its material presence is foregrounded and which evokes close engagement with surface detail and texture" (Kuhn & Westwell, 2012, p. 201). Films are powerful therapeutic tools to treat repressed experiences and emotions as they can be used to conjure up traumatic memories that our conscious mind could not process but that were stored in our bodies. As film theorist Laura Marks points out, "all of us hold knowledge in our bodies and memories in our senses" (Marks, 2000, p. xiii). It is not by chance that body psychotherapy, an embodied and integral approach to psychotherapy developed in the 1980s, has become increasingly popular because of its easier access to traumatic memories than the traditional psychoanalytic approach allows.

The Center for Digital Storytelling

As discussed in Chapter 14, the emergence of digital technologies in the 1990s provided film scholars, film students, and cinephiles alike with new tools to experiment with cinematic language to tell a story. Dana Atchley, Joe Lambert, and Nina Mullen decided to embrace this opportunity afforded by digital technology and in 1994 founded the San Francisco Digital Media Center to develop and lead community workshops under the rubric of "digital storytelling." Four years later, the Center moved to Berkeley as the Center for Digital Storytelling, and in 2015 the organization was renamed once again becoming the StoryCenter (Figure 15.1). Throughout the years, Lambert, Mullen, and Atchley (who died of complications from a bone marrow transplant in 2000), have helped heal personal traumas and support social justice through "the acts of listening to and sharing stories," transforming "the way that community activists, educators, health and human services agencies, business professionals, and artists think about the power of personal voice, in creating change" (StoryCenter, para. 4). In a nutshell, the StoryCenter staff employ digital storytelling as a pedagogical tool, as an instrument for social mobilization and political advocacy, and as a creative practice that encourages self-awareness and facilitates personal growth and healing.

The Y.O.U.T.H. Training Project

Founded in 2000, the Y.O.U.T.H. Training Project (YTP) (Figure 15.2) is an organization committed to empower transition-age foster youth (age 16–24) by training them to lead workshops with child welfare professionals. By teaching transition-age foster youth specialized skills in the child welfare sector, the

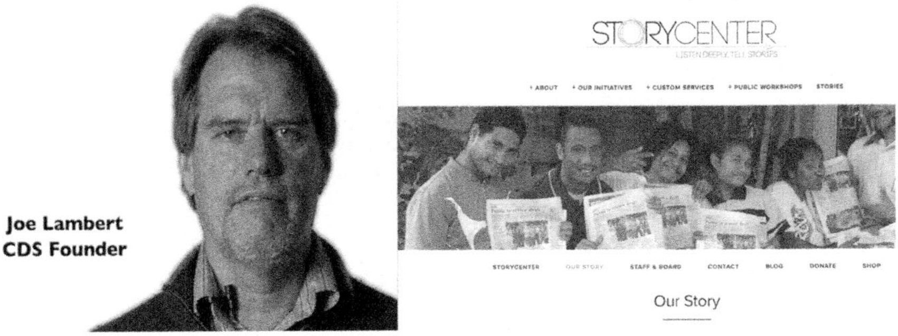

FIGURE 15.1 *Joe Lambert, founder of the Center for Digital Storytelling (now StoryCenter) www.storycenter.org/press./*

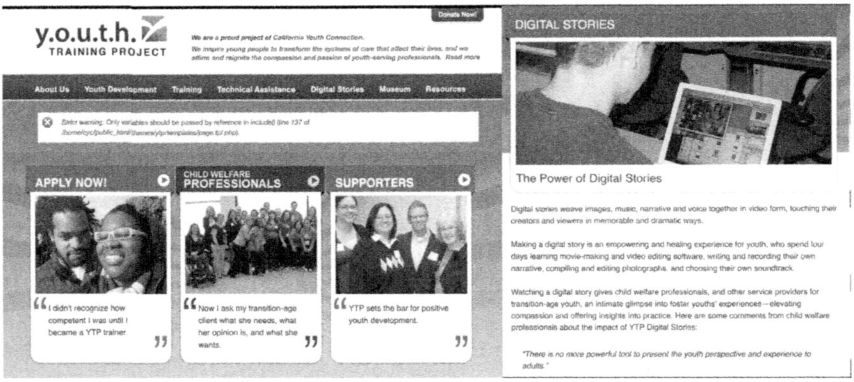

FIGURE 15.2 *The Y.O.U.T.H. Training Project http://youthtrainingproject.org/.*

YTP contributes to boosting their confidence and refining their interpersonal and communication competences. As the YTP website maintains, "In our Training programs, our empowered youth trainers draw from their experiences as consumers of the child welfare system to deliver potent training to child welfare professionals, with immediate applicability" (YTP website). And it is by reposing trust in foster youth and giving them leadership roles, that the YTP strengthens their confidence and self-esteem, contributing to their mental and physical health. To achieve these goals, the YTP's programs often incorporate Digital Storytelling activities into their training.

Sample Digital Stories from StoryCenter

www.storycenter.org/stories/

Nonclinical versus Clinical Cinematherapy

According to the American Mental Health Foundation, cinematherapy involves working with a trained film therapist, either individually or in a group setting, who can use film either for healing purposes or for general health and prevention. Indeed, there is an important distinction between nonclinical film therapy and film therapies done by a licensed practitioner or professional organizations such as the StoryCenter and the YTP. The following list serves to clarify that distinction.

Nonclinical Film Therapy

- Discussing your interpretation of a film's content and stylistic approach with a classmate.

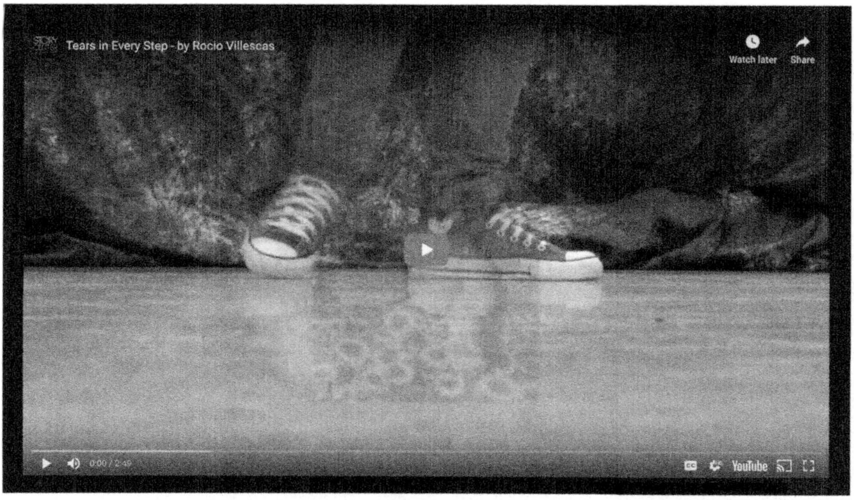

FIGURE 15.3 *TEARS IN EVERY STEP by Rocio Villescas (2012) www.youtube.com/watch?time_continue=4&v=FK10Ns9PY5o.*

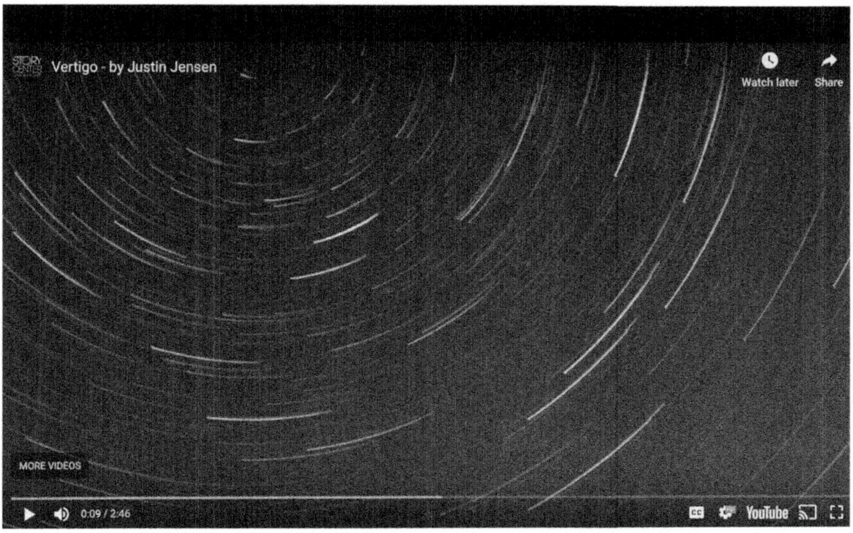

FIGURE 15.4 *VERTIGO by Justin Jensen (2018) www.youtube.com/watch?time_continue=9&v=QRNdmnbP8zs*

- Expressing your emotional response to a film to a friend and/or relative.
- Self-analyzing the psychological impact a movie had on you.
- Analyzing your friends' and/or relatives' emotional reactions to a film.
- Suggesting that a friend or relative watch a film you think will resonate with them emotionally, and then analyzing their responses.

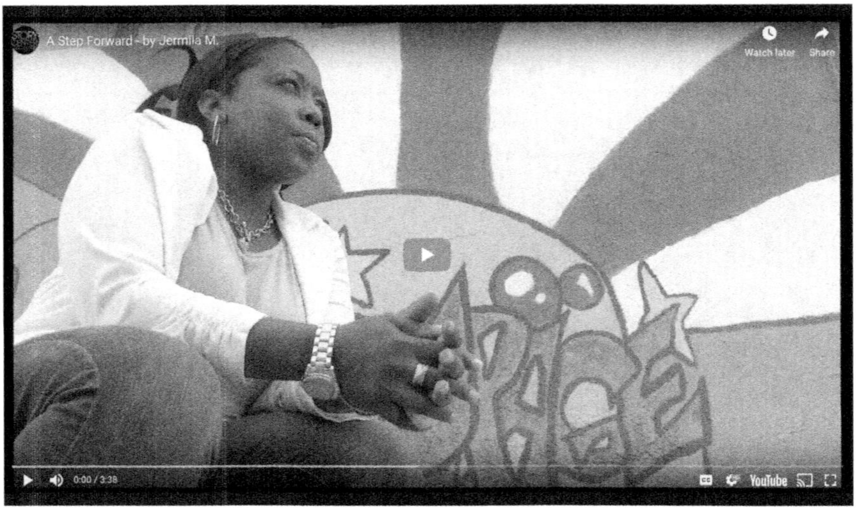

FIGURE 15.5 *A STEP FORWARD by Jermila M. (2015) www.youtube.com/watch?v=c_q8MdXgtrE*

Content Advisory: This story addresses the topic of rape. Viewers who are sensitive to the issue should watch at their own discretion.

Clinical Cinematherapy

- Healing from emotional trauma;
- Reducing anxiety and stress;
- Healing from physical abuse;
- Fostering children's and teens' self-esteem;
- Overcoming anorexia nervosa;
- Treating specific phobias such as social phobia and animal phobia;
- Curing post-traumatic stress disorder.

Movies Related to Mental-Health Themes

The Cinematherapy Film Index offers a comprehensive list of films related to the following mental-health themes:

- Inspiration;
- personal issues;
- social issues;
- children issues;
- adolescent issues;
- family issues;
- couple issues;

- mental and emotional illness;
- physical illness;
- medical issues.

Be sure to browse the list of films that Professor Birgit Wolz (2013) put together drawing from several professional sources (www.cinematherapy.com/filmindex.html).

Sample Abstracts Submitted to NCUR

www.cur.org/conferences_and_events/student_events/ncur/archive/

SENSE OF SELF: AN EXPLORATION OF PERSONAL IDENTITY IN MODERN FILM

Jason A Beck (Dr Christopher Hoyt), Department of Philosophy & Religion, Western Carolina University, Cullowhee, North Carolina 28723

Identity is defined as the sense of self, providing sameness and continuity in personality over time and sometimes disturbed in mental illnesses, as schizophrenia. According to John Locke, a 17th century philosopher, our consciousness is always shifting. We are born with a clean slate and the events we experience via sense perception and experience determine who we are and who we will become. As our consciousness shifts, so does our sense of self. We can use examples from film noir to help define identity and consciousness as seen in the real world. Andrew Spicer's interpretation of *Memento* points out that in order to have an identity, a person's memory and sense of time must be intact. He is specifically talking about a character with mental illness. If we take Spicer's ideas from his interpretation of *Memento* and compare them to yet another contemporary film, *Fight Club*, we will see more complexity in our concept of personal identity. I will use what Spicer has already said in order to clarify a further insight: There are certain social restrictions placed on us that limit the design of our true identity, and it is because of these limitations that we attempt to create a false identity. There is more here than just a comparison between two films. My paper will discuss philosophical concerns of the nature of personal identity and existential themes concerning self-awareness. The protagonists from both of these films are struggling to connect to the real world, and both must create a false self to make sense of their lives.

THE BOY WHO DESIRES ROLLER COASTERS: A DOCUMENTARY ABOUT ASPERGER SYNDROME

Kymberly Dixon (Deborah Jordan) Theatre Department, Jacksonville University, Jacksonville, Florida 32211

Since the 20th century, researchers have fought for Asperger Syndrome to be declared a separate category of autism. Hans Asperger was the original doctor to detect the syndrome in young boys who found it difficult to "fit in" socially with the other students. In 1944, Asperger wrote a research paper based on the autistic psychopathies in childhood. In his paper he described the hardships of these young men and their circumstances living with Aspergers. My inspiration to research Asperger Syndrome is my mentor's son. I was exposed to his condition and decided to make a subjective documentary about Asperger Syndrome. This documentary will outline the intimate aspects of this individual living with Asperger Syndrome. The significance of this story is to acknowledge all of the individuals experiencing adversity because of Asperger Syndrome. My goal is to communicate the personal story of this specific individual and should cause audience members to better understand Asperger Syndrome or other forms of Autism. The lens of my video camera captures the essential stories from many who are involved with this young man. I will demonstrate to the viewers, with a brief video clip, the technical features of producing a documentary which includes interviewing, bringing the camera into the world of the individual, and captivating music. The video implements being utilized for this documentary consist of a variety of camera angles, cinematography, script of questions and finalizing software such as Final Cut Pro.

FACING OUR FEARS: HOW *JACOB'S LADDER* SETS OUT TO RESOLVE THE REPRESSED

Author: Dustin Ledford Advisor: Dr. Barbara Brickman Department: Dept. of English & Philosophy Institution: University of West Georgia Institutional Address: 1600 Maple Street Carrollton, GA 30118

While horror has always had a psychological element to it, through addressing fears and issues of repression, the advent of psychological horror films like *Jacob's Ladder* brings with it a greater fusion between psychology and literature (Lynne, 1990). Due to this fusion psychological horror sets out with the intent to do more than just bring the repressed to the surface as the typical horror film does: it intends to resolve the conflict which the repressed creates. Unfortunately, the limited critical research available on this particular film means that this research project must construct its own critical reading based upon existing theories of the genre and psychoanalytic repression. One of the most commonly occurring conflicts comes out of a fear which society does not want to address, and perhaps the most frequently addressed of those is the fear of death and of "a non-corporeal or subhuman existence" (Wells, 10). While this fear of death or nonexistence has a presence in movies ranging from *Invasion of the Body Snatchers* to *The Texas Chainsaw Massacre, Jacob's Ladder* takes it on directly by first drawing the viewer into the nightmares of Jacob Singer, a man who straddles the border between life and death after being stabbed in Vietnam. Jacob's existence quickly becomes hellish as he deals with visions of demons, attacks on his life, and the confusion of slipping between lives with no understanding of where he is or why. As the film continues however, Jacob finally gains a sense of understanding and acceptance, embracing his fate and peacefully moving on to whatever is to come. *Jacob's Ladder* encourages a different kind of resolution than that offered by other horror films, opting to embrace and accept the repressed and confront it properly rather than leaving it a solely antagonistic force.

MEDIA'S OBSESSION WITH TRAGEDY: ARE WE HELPING OR HURTING VICTIMS THROUGH COVERAGE?

Author: Caroline Kim Faculty Mentor: George Yanez Department: Film and Visual Studies/English, Creative Writing Institution: George Mason University Address: 4400 University Drive Fairfax, VA 22030

According to the media, coverage of tragic events such as Sandy Hook and the Aurora shootings is necessary in order to spread awareness of said tragedies and to attract viewers to their stations. With the help of my mentor, George Yanez, I wrote, directed, and edited "Trans: A Short Film", a fictional documentary in which two videographers attempted to discover the effects of a neighborhood shooting and through their naivete, created unintended consequences. At first the videographers believe that the documentary will not be affecting anyone, because it is created out of curiosity. However, they are quickly proven wrong as they interview more and more victims. Some of these consequences were negative, such as agitating friends of victims as they grieved, or having the family members lie about the victim in order to depict her in a better light. However, some of these consequences benefitted the victims, because the documentary allowed them to come to terms with the deaths of their loved ones. In conclusion, the media can have both effects, negative and positive, depending on how the victim reacts to public grieving. However, it is not fair to assume that the media's invasiveness is always welcome during a tragedy, especially one that involves death.

CLOSING THE GAP BETWEEN KNOWLEDGE AND PRACTISE IN STROKE REHABILITATION USING ONLINE MEDIA

Author: Hayley Young Faculty Mentor: Louise Connell Department: School of Health Institution: University of Central Lancashire Institution Address: University of Central Lancashire, Preston, Lancashire, PR1 2HE

Objective: The objective was to design and develop a short online video to promote a stroke rehabilitation project. It aimed at enthusing patients, family, physiotherapists and occupational therapists about the development of a structured upper limb exercise programme, which can be feasibly implemented in stroke rehabilitation units in the United Kingdom. Background:

Demand for universities to demonstrate the impact of their research is now becoming a pre-requisite for successful funding applications. The National Institute for Health Research (NIHR) is the largest UK funder of applied health research and they recently launched a media competition to highlight their commitment to increasing the reach and impact of research. This media competition was open to NIHR funded researchers and aimed at producing a short video to motivate patients, colleagues, family and the public about the research and communicating research to the intended audiences. Methods: The developmental phase consisted of a review of existing on-line media for health research which informed the video content and format. Data was collected by scoping existing health media formats, which included reviewing literature in the field of social media platforms (i.e., Facebook, Twitter, YouTube, and Vimeo). Social media strategies, readership figures based on view counts, posts, likes and shares were collated. Specific health and stroke related websites were also searched to help develop an online campaign strategy and conduct relevant market research. Development of the video was conducted in a "point of view" perspective in order to relate to the audience and build up a sense of relationship between the viewer and the on-screen content. 30 volunteer participants performed simple everyday tasks using their hands and arms, producing over 100 individual video clips. The content of the video aimed to produce a strong underlining message that showed how often we use our hands and arms, relating this to stroke rehabilitation to highlight the on-going importance of rehabilitating the upper limbs. The video was piloted and adapted following feedback from stroke researchers, clinicians and the public to ensure the message was conveyed clearly. Results: The video was successfully produced and submitted into the NIHR's media competition on YouTube and currently has 630 view counts (www.youtube.com/watch?v=CqA3eey0xTQ). However as the competition is still running we are expecting figures to rise. The video is also now listed as the top search result on Google for the term "practise project". Conclusion: The development of an online video successfully increased the profile of the research, expanding the reach of the project. With the drive to demonstrate impact of research and increase public engagement, the use of online technology is a format that warrants further use and evaluation.

THE COLLAPSE OF THE FETISH: JEANNE DIELMAN AND PSYCHOANALYSIS

Booth Owens (Dr. Kristi McKim), Film Studies Department, Hendrix College, Conway, Arkansas

Rarely do films strain a spectator's patience like *Jeanne Dielman, 23 Quai du Commerce, 1080 Bruxelles* (Chantal Akerman, 1975). With a runtime of over 201 minutes and set over three full days, the film unfolds before the spectator like water set to boil. Despite the mundane routines of the protagonist, Jeanne

Dielman (actor) (Delphine Seyrig), the film finds a way to captivate the spectator. The film stylistically follows the theories of Christian Metz in his article, "Identification, Mirror," in which he states that the cinema shows the spectator great "perceptual wealth" through realistic imaging techniques, but denies the spectator a physical presence with the objects shown. Like the fetish, the apparent realism of Jeanne Dielman disavows the lack, and in so doing, affirms it. The techniques which Jeanne Dielman employs allow the spectator to trust the illusion of film, but their quiet presence weighs on the illusion. The static camera, the long take, and the absence of non-diegetic sound constitute the spectator's perception of reality, and, I will argue, affirm the lack. The fiction of the film which necessitates these techniques becomes more apparent with their implementation. The spectator, suddenly aware of the fiction which she observes, sees the collapse of the fetish when Jeanne Dielman murders a client after sex. I will argue that in the face of this violent act, the spectator can no longer believe the illusion that the fetish offers, because the film does not clearly justify the protagonist's actions. The spectator must intellectualize the film, disrupting the illusion of the cinema, and therefore, the fetish. In this way, Jeanne Dielman captivatingly pushes the limits of the cinema as a fetish, mobilizing every practical technique in order to bolster this fetish as a method of demolishing it, and therefore, proving it useless.

Conclusion

The medical profession is becoming increasingly aware of the benefits of cinematherapy and digital storytelling as they have been aiding people of all ages with a variety of conditions, greatly improving their lives and helping them reduce the number of medicines that they need for their conditions. Cinematherapy is also developing into a prominent field of study, holding promise for both qualitative and quantitative undergraduate research. By studying how films make us feel and connect us to each other, undergraduate students can greatly contribute to the film psychology scholarship.

Questions for Discussion

- Are we hardwired to like film?
- What technological advances are changing film and its effect on the psyche?
- How can film be used for healing?
- What is the history of cinematherapy?
- What are the statistics on the different conditions treated with cinematherapy?
- How does film give us an emotional, embodied experience?
- How can watching films help us make a connection in our community?

References

Adler, J. (2002). *Offering from the conscious body: The discipline of authentic movement*. Rochester, VT: Inner Traditions.

Clyman, J. (2013, Feb. 27). Cinematherapy: A useful tool in group therapy. *Psychology Today*. Retrieved from www.psychologytoday.com/us/blog/reel-therapy/201302/cinematherapy-useful-tool-in-group-therapy.

Cohen, J. L., Johnson, J. L., & Orr, P. P. (2015). *Video and filmmaking as psychotherapy: Research and practice*. New York: Routledge.

Kuhn, A. & Westwell, G. (2012). *A dictionary of film studies*. Oxford: Oxford University Press.

Marks, L. U. (2000). *The skin of the film: Intercultural cinema, embodiment, and the senses*. Durham, NC: Duke University Press.

StoryCenter. (n.d.). How it all began. *Our Story*. Retrieved from www.storycenter.org/press/.

Wolz, B. (2005). *E-Motion picture magic: A movie lovers guide to healing and transformation*. Centennial, CO: Glenbridge Publications.

Wolz, B. (2013). Cinematherapy film index. Retrieved from www.cinematherapy.com/filmindex.html.

Y.O.U.T.H. Training Project. (2016). The power of digital stories. Retrieved from http://youthtrainingproject.org/?q=digital_stories.

16

CINEMA, CULTURE, AND SOCIETY

I think you always need the double perspective. Before you say that you have to understand what it is like to come from that "other" place. How it feels to live in that closed world. How such ideas have kept people together in the face of all that has happened to them. But you also have to be true to your own culture of debate and you have to find some way to begin to translate between those two cultures. It is not easy, but it is necessary.

Stuart Hall

The news, the media, the Internet, the global marketplace—it has never been clearer that in our times, we are players in a theater of dynamic social forces.

Mary Lynn Kittelson

Documentary is about arranging and telling stories, not about delivering objective truth.

Hayden White

Cinema is unique in that it is a highly accessible social art form, the participation in which generally cuts across economic line.

Vikas S. Shah

Summary

Cinema has been interpreted as a mirror of society, since films usually reflect the cultures, social attitudes, and belief systems of their producers. Films tend to operate as some sort of allegory, teaching us something about life, providing us with moral lessons and answers to existential questions. With the aid of digital technology, now films from all over the world are available to watch online or on cable television. This opportunity to be exposed to foreign films gives us a glimpse into people, customs, and traditions from other countries and cultures, broadening our worldview. This chapter examines the relationship between filmmakers and the cultural and social influences that impact their films' message and stylistic approach. Influential directors and films representing diverse style periods, cultures and subcultures, and historical backgrounds will be discussed. Sample projects and abstracts will show students the breadth of possibilities in these areas of research.

Film and International Culture

Cinema is a relatively new medium, patented at the very end of the 19th century. Over its 120 years of existence, the moving camera has either documented or dramatized major social transitions, political crises, and tragic events, including an international economic depression, the process of decolonization, ethnic genocides and diasporas, global wars, student and working-class protests, and cultural and technological revolutions. Whether funded privately or by state government, film coverage of these major global occurrences has been widely disseminated through the big screen and the small screen, and, since the 1990s, via the internet.

Any understanding of contemporary global societies must examine the huge impact that cinematic representation has on them and their cultural expression, and, at the same time, how filmic representation itself expresses those societies' cultural values and beliefs. The possibilities for undergraduate research in the subject area of film and international culture are almost endless. Perhaps a faculty member teaching at your academic institution is from a foreign country, or maybe you have watched foreign films and/or learned to make films while studying abroad. Or what about interviewing international exchange students at your university? Many filmmakers around the world have been inspired to introduce international stylistic conventions into their films. Examples abound, such as Italian neorealism's influence on Indian and Latin American cinema (e.g., Satyajit Ray's *Pather Panchali*, 1955; Alfonso Cuarón's *Roma*, 2018), German Expressionism's significant impact on the birth of the film noir and horror genres in the US, or Darren Aronofsky's use of soviet montage techniques in his American film production *Requiem for a Dream* (2000).

Film and Local Culture

Between the 1930s and the early 1990s, the Hollywood film industry had been a major disseminator of Western values and culture worldwide, contributing to shaping the global collective imaginary from a traditional Caucasian middle-class perspective. Over the past three decades, however, American cultural imperialism has been increasingly challenged by the rise of independent cinemas within Western societies, the widespread distribution of foreign films worldwide, and the advent of the internet, especially the creation of Web 2.0, which emphasizes user-generated content. In the information age, the dissemination of localized and indigenous knowledges, dissenting discourses, and personal stories via the World Wide Web has been a crucial determinant in undermining the process cultural homogenization from a Western perspective. This means that there are limitless opportunities for undergraduate film students to perform research that focuses on the local and the regional. Which cultures and subcultures are represented around you? What kinds of films tend to be screened in your town's movie theaters? Which film events are showcased near you? Which venues serve as film hubs? Do you know of any local filmmakers who have challenged mainstream assumptions about effective storytelling strategies? This is just a small sample of the boundless opportunities for film undergraduate research at a local level.

Documentary Film and Society

By the 1930s, Hollywood cinematic style was well established, becoming the most popular fiction filmmaking approach in the Western world. The challenges posed by the international economic depression, however, also created a demand for films that could inform their viewers of contemporary sociopolitical issues and provide a solution to those problems. Hollywood cinema's entertaining value was not suited to addressing such somber matters adequately. John Grierson, a British scholar expert in the sociology of propaganda, coined what Western film historians consider the first definition of documentary filmmaking, *the creative treatment of actuality*, describing it as a realistic and "objective" portrayal of everyday life (Kerrigan & McIntyre, 2010). In the 21st century, more and more filmmakers are rejecting the idea that documentary films are "objective" representation of reality, incorporating fictional techniques such as reenactments and animation in their nonfiction films to illustrate aspects of life that would be impossible to record in live action. Contemporary documentarians are also increasingly replacing the overarching narratives offered by the traditional documentary approach (i.e., Grierson) with micronarratives that emphasize differences over similarities, dissent over consensus, recognizing the importance of localized knowledge in the search for social truths.

Be inspired to discover the social and cultural realities of your own town as potential subjects for your documentary film project. For example, you could visit the local homeless shelter and interview people experiencing homelessness to raise awareness about their condition and the need to support them in your community. Alternatively, you could either conduct vox pop interviews with community members attending the local farmer market asking whether they practice composting or create a film portrayal of young adults who struggle with mental illness to help raise funding for mental health services in your town. There is a multiplicity of potential subjects to choose from at the local level for helping community advocacy. Documentary film is indeed a powerful tool for activism and social change (see Chapter 10 for social justice documentary projects at the local level).

Fieldwork as a Process of Research

How does one conduct research of a community's film-viewing patterns? This process is referred to as fieldwork. After preliminary research of a community's movie theaters, for example, fieldwork requires the researcher to go to the local film venues and events to observe, interview, and record, and then to report back. The goal as the participant is cultural immersion and becoming an active observer—you are in the audience, experiencing films as the people of that community experience them. Take detailed notes as the participant observer, interview the movie goers and, when possible, the filmmakers. Fieldwork research may be conducted anywhere at any kind of event for any kind of film screening. Interest in a regional film festival may lead a fieldworker to attend the event, participating as much as possible, interviewing other participants, and recording the experience through the camera. Participating as an audience member of a film screening, speaking with the filmmaker's fans, and researching the fan base all constitute as fieldwork.

Interpretation of the world around us will inevitably be colored by our position as observers. Coming from our various cultures and contexts, the task of comprehending another culture's worldview is a difficult and complex one. This tension between objectivity and bias from our own cultural production is commonly referred to as "cultural relativism." Although "objectivity" is simply unattainable, fieldworkers must interact as directly as possible with a culture to begin to understand the peoples that they are studying. Film libraries and collections abound for us to begin the eye-opening adventure of watching a film produced in a foreign culture and hopefully learning to appreciate different cinematic styles and cultural understandings of the world. What movies did you grow up watching? Have you ever been exposed to films from other cultures? How did they affect you? Did they change (or reaffirm) your own viewpoint?

Possible Topics

- Interview international students who are attending film programs in the United States and ask them how they perceive the differences between Western mainstream filmmaking and the film culture in their country.
- Explore how studying another country's culture can inform the analysis of the films which that country produces.
- Compare the filmmaking stylistic conventions that are popular within another culture with Western mainstream cinema's aesthetic.

- Analyze the ways in which a given country's filmmaking style is incorporated into Hollywood cinema.
- Interview local filmmakers about international influences in their film productions.
- Study the governmental support for mainstream filmmaking in various countries and compare/contrast them.
- Research governmental censure and its effect on the films of certain directors.
- Analyze Western influences on the Bollywood filmmaking approach.
- Find a cultural center that partners with local filmmakers and investigate its impact in the community.
- Interview teenagers at local film events and research their favorite movies to assess local filmmaking trends.
- Examine the impact of digital technology on the local versus the global film culture.
- Conduct interviews with the local homeless population and staff members from that community's human resource development center to find out their needs.
- Apply a community-based participatory research framework to perform a documentary project about the availability of mental health services in a rural community of your choice.

Sample Abstracts Submitted to NCUR

www.cur.org/conferences_and_events/student_events/ncur/archive/

DIFFERENT NAMES FOR THE SAME THING: APPROPRIATION OF GERMANIC NAMES IN THE ROCKY HORROR PICTURE SHOW

Author—Harold Richard Collins III, Advisor-Dr. Barbara Brickman, The University of West Georgia at 1601 Maple St, Carrollton, GA 30118.

Jim Sharman's 1975 film "*The Rocky Horror Picture Show*" uses a variety of tropes from the American horror genre to new ends as it parodies American horror and comments on preconceived notions of foreignness in small town America. Interestingly, references to Germany—specifically through manipulations of Germanic names—remains one of the most prevalent and consistent foreign elements throughout. Through Brad's introduction of Janet to Frankfurter, Frankfurter's revelation of the "von" in the middle of Dr. Scott's name, and the Americanization of Frankfurter's name into "hotdog" reveal assimilation into American culture through manipulations of names. I will discuss each of these scenes in my presentation through individual shots and also reveal that the fear with which these characters react when approached with the German version of their names illustrates an anxiety of being found out as foreign and, in the case of Dr. Scott, being tied with the Nazi party in a post WWII

America. I will also explain how these Germanic references ultimately illustrate a reversal of the fears tied with foreignness—illustrated in the first vampire film "*Nosferatu*" (Murnau 1922), the cold war film "*Invasion of the Body Snatchers*" (Siegel 1956), and through Brad Majors in "*Rocky Horror*"—and ultimately reveals a liberation for Janet, Brad, and Dr. Scott at the hand of 'transsexual aliens from the galaxy Transylvania' ("*Rocky Horror*"). In this way, the film continues its parody of the horror genre and comments on egocentric Americans, such as Brad, who would normally dismiss those people outside America as simply 'foreigners with ways different from our own' ("*The Rocky Horror Picture Show*").

FAMILY IDEOLOGY IN 21ST CENTURY SPANISH CINEMA

Nicole C Weinstock, Esther Yau, Department of Art History and the Visual Arts—Film and Media Studies Division, Occidental College, 1600 Campus Rd, Los Angeles, CA 90041

This study examines various aspects of family ideology in two recent Spanish films. *The Sea Inside* (Alejandro Amenábar, 2004), bases itself in the true story of quadriplegic Ramon Sampedro and his unsuccessful legal battle for "death with dignity." The film emphasizes his relationships with various women who look to him for love, friendship, comfort and a more appealing representation of masculinity. *Take My Eyes* (Iciar Bollaín, 2003) focuses on the reality of domestic violence in Spain through its depiction of Pilar's struggle for independence from her abusive husband Antonio, traditional mother and progressive sister. Using a Lacanian lens and theoretical support from Kaja Silverman's study of post-World War II cinema, I investigate how the dominant fiction functions in these two films. The dominant fiction reinforces the male's imaginary relation to the phallus. It therefore prevents him from encountering his own lack granted there are no historically traumatic experiences. *The Sea Inside* and *Take My Eyes* however, do imply the occurrence of a traumatic historic episode, the liberation of women during the post-Franco era of democracy. The films then illustrate the different ways in which men react to this trauma and resultant encounter with lack: some men like Antonio deny their evident lack, while others like Ramon are written to embrace it. While the former reinforce existing family ideology, the latter transcend the more traditional biological notions of family. They not only suggest the validity of nonbiological surrogate relations, but they redefine 21st century Spanish masculinity through lack and perceived disability.

HOLDING UP THE MIRROR: CULTURAL VALUES AND PERCEPTIONS REFLECTED IN DISNEY ANIMATION

Wesam D. Abdeljabbar (Bonnie Orzolek) Department of English, Virginia Commonwealth University, Richmond, VA 23284

Most people mistakenly consider the entertainment medium of animation to be nothing more than a genre designed to keep children occupied. Thus, it is uncommon to find people reflecting seriously on the relationship between Disney animation and American culture. This is unfortunate, since analyzing the content within Disney animation can provide useful tools to help understand the kind of values that Americans hold and how they view the world. The prevailing view among most of those who criticize the entertainment industry, such as Henry Giroux and Mia Towbin, is that Disney, with all of its popularity and marketing power, molds the views and attitudes of the nation's young people. The purpose of this study is to see if this criticism is legitimate. The scope of the research was focused on the films that were produced by Walt Disney Animation Studios (formerly known as Walt Disney Feature Animation) and, to a lesser extent, Pixar Animation Studios. The scholarship of cultural critics was utilized to study the analysis of the portrayal of different groups. Such portrayals include representations of various races and ethnicities, portrayals of women, etc. The conclusion that arose out of examining the evidence mentioned is that although Disney animation is accused of sending subtle messages to influence its audience, the popular ethos of society at large influences the cultural values that Disney portrays. The major implication of such a conclusion is that it casts doubt on the criticisms of those who say that animation is brainwashing children in to holding certain views and values. If society desires for animation companies to modify the values that they portray, then change must come from the society itself.

POLITICAL REFORM AS A DISEASE FOR THE FAMILY INSTITUTION: THE REPRESENTATION OF COMMUNISM AS EVIL IN *YELLOW EARTH*

Diana R. Duarte (Greta Niu) Department of English, University of Rochester, Rochester, NY 14627

This research paper analyzes the portrayal of communism as a hostile environment for the institution of family in the film *Yellow Earth* (PRC 1984, directed by Chen Kaige). Communism challenges the father's power as the head of household, and ruins the lives of the youth due to its volatile nature with traditional Chinese rural life. *Yellow Earth* depicts China's clash of communism against rural life as a struggle between modernity versus tradition. Brother Gu represents modernity, an officer sent by the newly established communist regime to collect songs of the rural peasantry (tradition). Other aspects of traditional life besides music are the farmers' conventions of family structure and marriage. The ending scenes of *Yellow Earth* suggest that modernity in the form of communism cannot co-exist with tradition, creating a radical and destructive force that extends itself to the most personal of relationships, the institution of family. The scenes that appear to validate the image of a family being torn apart are Brother Gu's general attitude on rejecting tradition, Cuiqiao's last song, and the end of the rain dance when Brother Gu returns to Shaanxi Province. These scenes, with a combination of specific cinematography techniques, create an unsettling experience. Guiding my scene analyses is Benjamin's "*The Work of Art in the Age of Mechanical Reproduction*" and his idea of film being "mentally intrusive", and is a tool to establish political ideas by using "experience". Directing my argument on communism as a threat to the institution of family is Leung's "Yellow Earth: Hesitant Apprenticeship and Bitter Agency", Marx and Engels' *Communist Manifesto*, and Kollontai's "*Communism and the Family*".

POSTHUMAN ETHNOGRAPHY

Adam G. Hughes (Luca Caminati) Film & Media Studies Program, Colgate University, Hamilton, NY 13346

The legacy of colonial anthropology colors all filmic representations of the Other. While documentary ethnography has been defined as "any film which seeks to reveal one society to another," (MacDougall, "Prospects of the Ethnographic Film") to actually reveal the "truth" of a society is an impossible goal. The meaning an outsider assigns to a representation cannot be objective nor comprehensive due to the gap between the real and its representation—the process of recording necessarily obscures that which lies beyond the frame. Yet many ethnographic documentaries profess to tell the objective truth, to describe a people or culture in rational terms so that viewers can be made to completely understand what they are watching. I argue that this premise is a fallacy, and that a completely objective ethnographic film must necessarily fictionalize its subject. Luis Buñuel's 1933 film *Land Without Bread* (Las Hurdes) depicts Los Hurdanos, an isolated group that lives in the mountains of central Spain (Las Hurdes). The narrator blatantly lies and manipulates viewers, while brutally insulting the subjects. Spatial and temporal continuity is ignored. By drawing attention to these representational breaches the viewer must reassess their privileged position, and revaluate their comprehension of the depicted. Jørgen Leth's 1967 film *The Perfect Human* (*Det Perfekte Menneske*) also interrupts ethnographic discourse through fictional subjects, surrealist mise-en-scène, and an abrasive and repetitive narrator. I argue that each film represents objectivity precisely through the totality of its dishonesty. By eroding the viewer's subject-identification, both *Land Without Bread* and *The Perfect Human* reveal the impossibility of ethnographic objectivity. Illogical narrative, hazy spatial representation, and unconventional narration serve to alienate any epistephilic viewer, who must then confront his or her own demand for truth.

ANIME: WINDOW TO THE JAPANESE IDENTITY

Elise M. Isom (Bonnie Orzolek), Honors College, Virginia Commonwealth University, Richmond, VA 23220

The contemporary artist and scholar of Japanese society, Takashi Murakami, believes that certain elements of Japan's culture serve as "windows" onto the inner workings of the Japanese persona. These windows can include music, fashion, film, or specific expressions and behaviors. Like many modern scholars of Japan, Murakami has noticed the substantial change that Japan has experienced in its post-war period. While Japan appears to be completely recovered from the atomic destruction of its past, under the serene exterior an accelerating cultural struggle and sense of misplaced identity exist. With bombs on Hiroshima and Nagasaki in August of 1945, Japan has experienced apocalyptic conditions unlike any other country on earth. The haunting devastation has left an irreversible stigma; what had existed before was erased and Japan was given a new beginning as a nation left to find itself again in a modern world. After the war came the flood of Westernization, during which came the true birth of the Japanese animation industry. The increasing success and prevalence of anime makes it the cultural symbol of Japan. Anime serves as an appropriate window onto the problems that Japan faces with its national identity in relation to culture, values, gender, and generation due to its deep integration and widespread popularity in Japanese society. As an example, this study considers the anime films of the esteemed Japanese animator and filmmaker Hayao Miyazaki. Miyazaki uses his films to bring to light the major issues of Japanese society and to create a sense of awareness. By analyzing his major films, the many aspects that make up the Japanese identity crisis are exposed and the validity of anime as a reflection of cultural conditions is substantiated.

SINCERE MISSIONS, CULTURAL EXTINCTIONS

Jadon Marianetti (Dr. Don Wagner and Dr. Christopher Aanstoos) Department of Political Science, Honors College, University of West Georgia 1601 Maple St. Carrollton, GA 30118

Chinua Achebe's novel *Things Fall Apart* and Bruce Beresford's film *Black Robe* create a fascinating dialogue regarding the importance and sincerity of Christian missionaries during the peak of European colonialism from a lens of cultural relativity. Achebe tells the story from the perspective of an African tribal leader watching his tribe fall apart as a result of the new religions influence. In *Black Robe*, the protagonist is a Jesuit priest who ventures deep into native land in an attempt to save heathen souls. Thus both mediums discuss incredibly similar topics from opposing perspectives. Though both the film and the novel certainly lament the loss of the indigenous cultures as a result of western imperialism, they both go through pain staking efforts to portray the Christian missionaries as completely sincere. Furthermore, both mediums take stances against both societies in support of cultural relativism. For example, in *Black Robe*, the camera flashes back and forth between a tribal ceremony and a catholic ritual (both looking eerily similar). Additionally, the Jesuit protagonist and his doppelganger, the tribal spiritual leader, are constantly enmeshed over competing (and equally reasonless) truth claims, such as calling each other a devil. In *Things Fall Apart*, Achebe purposely makes Okonkwo an unsympathetic chauvinistic protagonist in order to reflect simultaneously on both societies. Okonkwo's son converts to Christianity as a rejection of his culture's hyper masculinity despite its subsequent consequences for his society. Ultimately, despite the Missionaries altruistic intentions, they ultimately weakened and began the process of cultural extinction for the indigenous communities they encountered.

BRANAGH, THE BARD, AND THE BLITHE: HOW *MUCH ADO ABOUT NOTHING* PASSES IN CONTEMPORARY SOCIETY

Stephanie Zimmerman (Dr. Marcela Kostihová), Department of English, Hamline University, 1536 Hewitt Avenue, Saint Paul, Minnesota, 55104

Much Ado About Nothing is commonly renowned as one of Shakespeare's best comedies but has reappeared only rarely in the American film industry. According to Richard Burt's, the only cinematic version of the play to appear in the last twenty years is Kenneth Branagh's 1993 film of the same title. Critics of the adaptation seem to agree with startling consistency about the film's tone: William Brugger calls it a "sunny adaptation" that "warmed the hearts" while Neil McDonald calls it a "sunny, lighthearted interpretation," and both agree with the copy written on the back cover of MGM's DVD: a "sexy, sunny comedy." In fact, few critics address the adaptation's significance in terms of its effect on the play's meaning and impact. The film's deviations from the Shakespearean script are significant and in most cases have been well documented but not thoroughly examined or explored. Hal Hinson calls the film "insubstantial" and says it proves "in the wrong hands, even Shakespeare can be trivialized and reduced to chatter." Hinson's review begins to identify the ways the film glosses over moral and human complications in Shakespeare's play. Back stories are embellished or edited, characters' motives are blurred or constructed, and moments previously open to interpretation are filled in by Branagh's script. The film's omissions and alterations do more than lighten the backdrop; they fundamentally change (and simplify) the play by way of its characters' relationships and moral development. Through close examination of the adaptation and its critical and cultural reception, this study aims to correct these oversights and provides a fuller, more substantial critical reading of Branagh's production. The reception of Branagh's film highlights the ways a contemporary audience is willing to gloss over a more complicated exploration of human nature in favor of a brighter, simpler reflection of morality.

Conclusion

Much stands to be researched in terms of international and local film cultures and their relationship to the societies that produce them. The multiplicity of film styles and approaches within each society, culture, and subculture, and even within each person, provides film scholars and students with a fertile terrain for research. Advocacy documentary projects are especially suited for addressing local community issues, and contributing to undergraduate students' outreach and engagement activities.

Questions for Discussion

- How does our culture influence film?
- Why does it take so long for people to appreciate foreign and independent films?
- What film production roles do we designate as either "men's" or "women's?" Where do these views come from? How are they changing, if they are?
- What is "cultural relativism?"
- What is the difference between mainstream filmmaking and experimental cinema?
- What is cinema? To you? To your social group? To your nation?
- How does film influence culture? Politics? Young people's lives?

References

Hall, S. cited in Adams, T. (2007, Sep. 23). Cultural hallmark. *The Guardian*. Retrieved from www.theguardian.com/society/2007/sep/23/communities.politicsphilosophyandsociety.

Kerrigan, S., & McIntyre, P. (2010). The "creative treatment of actuality": Rationalizing and reconceptualizing the notion of creativity for documentary practice. *Journal of Media Practice*, *11*(2): 111–130.

Kittelson, M. L. (1998). *The soul of popular culture: Looking at contemporary heroes, myths, and monsters*. Chicago, IL: Open Court.

Shah, V. S. (2011, June 19). The role of film in society. *Thought Economics*. Retrieved from https://thoughteconomics.com/the-role-of-film-in-society/.

White, H. (1996). The modernist event. In Sobchack, V. (Ed.), *The persistence of history: Cinema, television, and the modern event* (pp. 17–38). New York: Routledge.

17

ONLINE RESOURCES

Summary

This chapter presents an annotated list of online resources with a short description about each to help students judge their credibility, usefulness, and relevance. It is divided up by category, with some adherence to the chapter headings in this book. Included are the NCUR Abstract Archives in Film, online writing labs and formatting guides, as well as links to numerous film resources available on the World Wide Web. Be aware that online resources are constantly changing, so you might be redirected to a different URL.

Resources for All Film Majors

National Conferences of Undergraduate Research (NCUR) have, since 1987, been archiving abstracts from the thousands of students who present each year and the database is searchable. https://ncurdb.cur.org/ncur2016/archive/Search_NCUR.aspx

The Society for Cinema and Media Studies Undergraduate (SCMS-U) Hub is a space dedicated to resources and announcements for film and media studies undergraduate students, and keeps them informed about the annual SCMS-U Conference dates and call for proposals.

www.cmstudies.org/page/undergraduate

Writing Commons is a free, comprehensive, peer-reviewed, award-winning open text for students and faculty in college-level courses that require writing and research. https://writingcommons.org/open-text/writing-processes/publish/1019-undergraduate-publishing-websites

UNL Libraries is an online guide containing information for undergraduates interested in publication. Journals are divided into categories with links to each. https://unl.libguides.com/c.php?g=51642&p=333910

The California Film Commission offers a vast array of tools and resources to help navigate all sorts of production issues, from work permits to on-set safety. Find links and contact info for relevant government agencies, industry associations, guilds and unions, production directories, entertainment job listings, and more. Find useful charts for studio zones weather and college locations to name a few. http://film.ca.gov/production/associations-guilds/

Filmmakers without Borders (FWB) is an educational nonprofit organization dedicated to empowering the next generation of digital storytellers. Through various grants, educational resources, and international fellowships, FWB provides youth from underserved communities with the technical training, media literacy skills, and digital tools to leverage the creative process as a means for interpreting their role in their society. http://filmmakerswithout borders.org/

PechaKucha 20x20 is a simple presentation format where you show 20 images, each for 20 seconds. The images advance automatically and you talk along to the images. www.pechakucha.org/watch

TED Talks offer a variety of fascinating talks on film and digital audiovisual media. These talks range in length from about 5–20 minutes and some have been viewed by over 40 million people.

www.ted.com/talks/

English and Media Centre is an independent educational charity with a national and international reputation as a Centre of Excellence. It is a development center, serving the needs of secondary and FE teachers and students of English and Media Studies in the UK and beyond.

www.englishandmedia.co.uk/

Cinemagic is an award-winning Northern Ireland-based charity and is the largest film and television festival designed for and by young people in the UK and Ireland. To date they have engaged with over 500,000 young people, screened over 3,000 films, and hosted over 500 master classes, workshops, and special events. Their film production projects have received international acclaim for their ambition, quality, and reach.

https://cinemagic.org.uk/

The National Science and Media Museum is a gallery space devoted to exploring the science and culture of image and sound technologies and their impact on our lives. The museum hosts world-famous collections in photography, film, and television, and has three cinema screens including an IMAX theatre, showing films from around the world.

www.scienceandmediamuseum.org.uk/

Film Studies for Free is a web-archive of examples of, links to, and comments on, online film and audiovisual media studies resources of note.

https://filmstudiesforfree.blogspot.com/2012/12/the-best-online-film-studies-resources.html

Digital Storytelling and Audiovisual Essay Resources

The StoryCenter Website is an online platform showcasing the StoryCenter's programs, workshops, and resources on digital storytelling. As the StoryCenter's mission statement explains, *we create spaces for transforming lives and communities, through the acts of listening to and sharing stories. Our public program enables people to register individually for storytelling workshops. Our custom program collaborates with organizations around the world, on workshops in story facilitation, digital storytelling, and other forms of participatory media production.*

www.storycenter.org/

The Audiovisual Essay Website is an online repository for the papers, discussions, and screening program of the international conference on *The Audiovisual Essay: Practice and Theory*, organized by Adrian Martin and Cristina Álvarez López in November 2013; a companion publication to issue 1.3 of the peer-reviewed journal *(in)Transition*, the first peer-reviewed academic periodical about videographic film and moving image studies; a rolling publication for continuing reflections on the practice and theory of the audiovisual essay; and a place of publication for resources about and guides to making and teaching about audiovisual essays.

http://reframe.sussex.ac.uk/audiovisualessay/

Audiovisualcy is an online forum for video essays or works of audiovisual screen studies that have an analytical, critical reflexive, or scholarly purpose.

https://vimeo.com/groups/audiovisualcy

The Best Video Essays of 2017 (*BFI*, December 2017) lists a curated selection of 33 audiovisual essays.

www.bfi.org.uk/news-opinion/sight-sound-magazine/polls-surveys/annual-round-ups/best-video-essays-2017

Article on Kagonada's Audiovisual Essays by Chris O'Falt (August 7, 2017) "How Video Essays Helped Kogonada Make One of the Most Exciting Debuts of 2017." *Indie Wire*.

www.indiewire.com/2017/08/columbus-kogonada-yasujiro-ozu-video-essay-filmmaker-toolkit-podcast-episode-38-1201863745/

Kagonada is a website featuring a curated selection of audiovisual essays by South Korean-born American filmmaker Kagonada.

http://kogonada.com/

Film Studies Resources

Film Studies Research Guide: Organizations & Associations lists organizations and associations that play a crucial role in advancing film criticism, production, preservation and scholarship.

https://guides.library.yale.edu/c.php?g=295800&p=1975081

Film Inquiry is a progressive, independent film magazine that aims to redefine film journalism. They publish in-depth, high quality articles written by a diverse group of people.

www.filminquiry.com/

Film Study Reference Guide: Film Theory and Criticism contains resources for theory, criticism, and history on film. While most of these sources are print, you can also access online sources through FIAF (International Federation of Film Archives). Hosted by the University of Illinois, Urbana-Champaign.

https://guides.library.illinois.edu/c.php?g=347540&p=2344064

Film Quarterly combines the best of scholarship and journalism since 1959 by publishing in-depth articles, reviews, and interviews on all aspects of cinema, media, and society—from film classics to emergent technologies. *Film Quarterly* is committed to advancing timely and intersectional approaches to the criticism and analysis of visual culture through exploring new perspectives on issues of diversity, race, gender, sexuality, and transnationalism.

https://filmquarterly.org/

***Encyclopedia Britannica* Definition of Film Theory**

www.britannica.com/art/film-theory

Interdisciplinary Resources

The Society for Cognitive Studies of the Moving Image (SCSMI) fosters interdisciplinary research within the areas of moving image history, theory, and aesthetics; cognitive science; and the philosophy of mind and art. The Society supports dialogue in all directions, so that every represented discipline may learn from the others. Through exchange, debate, and collaboration among moving image theorists, historians, analysts, philosophers, scientists, and artists, SCSMI promotes research into moving image media and the ways in which such media reflect, shape, and are shaped by the human mind.

http://scsmi-online.org/

H-Net is an interdisciplinary organization of scholars and teachers dedicated to developing the enormous educational potential of the internet and the World Wide Web. Their edited networks publish peer reviewed essays, multimedia materials, and discussions for colleagues and the interested public. The computing heart and main office of H-Net resides at the History Department, Michigan State University, but H-Net officers, editors, and subscribers come from all over the globe.

https://networks.h-net.org/

The Interdisciplinary Minor in Film Studies offers students the opportunity to select a program of study that explores the many facets of American and international films, the role of films in cultures, and hands-on film production.

The interdisciplinary nature of the program allows students to experience different approaches to film study: film and cultural differences, basic film vocabulary, film history, film and social forces, film genres, film theories, film directors, film aesthetics, film and performance, and film production.

www.uscb.edu/academics/academic_departments/school-of-humanities-and-social-sciences/english-theater-liberal-studies/liberal_studies/film-studies.html

Film Technology Resources

Article on New Technological Trends and Challenges in Cinema by Benjamin B (March 14, 2018) "Cinema 2018–9 Key Trends/Challenges." *American Cinematographer.*

https://ascmag.com/blog/the-film-book/cinema-2018-key-trends

Article on Recent Technological Advances that Revolutionized the Film Industry by Ángela Bernardo (March 10, 2016) "7 Advances in Technology that have Revolutionized the Film Industry." *OpenMind.*

www.bbvaopenmind.com/en/7-advances-in-technology-that-have-revolutionized-the-film-industry/

Article on Advances in Motion Capture and 3-D Printing by David Sheldon-Hicks (June 12, 2015) "Five Ways Film-Making Is Evolving Thanks to New Technology." *The Guardian.*

www.theguardian.com/culture-professionals-network/2015/jun/12/film-technology-evolution-film-making-3d-printing-vr-motion-capture

The Ultimate Animation Software List is a website that lists and introduces 55 top animation software for research topics related to computer 2-D and 3-D animation.

www.renderforest.com/blog/best-animation-software.

Film Education Resources

Classroom Resources for Film Teachers (BFI) is an online resource that supports teachers in introducing students to specialist, independent, and archive film by sharing knowledge, techniques, and critical approaches.

www.bfi.org.uk/education-research/teaching-film-tv-media-studies

Film & Video Workshop is a web resource that provides detailed advice on how to use their DVD in the classroom. It is adapted from the booklet that comes with the DVD and contains more up-to-date information and additional material and downloads. If you have been using this resource Film & Video Workshop would appreciate any feedback and any advice you might want to pass on to your colleagues in the form of lessons plans, etc.

www.filmworkshop.com/animagine-resources/

The Film Education Website promotes and supports the use of film within the curriculum.

www.filmeducation.org/

The Digital Storytelling Multimedia Archive shares the results of a multicampus study of student learning and digital storytelling in humanities classrooms. In this website you will find: (1) a research section addressing three major themes (multimedia distinctive, social pedagogy, and affective learning); (2) a grid that shows a condensed representation of the project's findings; and (3) video interviews with students and faculty that produced digital stories.

https://pilot.cndls.georgetown.edu/digitalstories/

The International Association of Film and Television Schools (*Centre International de Liaison des Ecoles de Cinéma et de Télévision*—CILECT) was founded in Cannes, France, in 1954 by Marcel L'Herbier (IDHEC President) and Rémy Tessonneau (IDHEC General Director) who, for the first time, gathered together higher education film school representatives from France, Italy, Poland, Spain, the UK, USA, and USSR. CILECT believes in the inherent interconnectivity of humankind and fully supports creativity, diversity, cross-cultural thinking, and sustainable development as fundamental prerequisites to human existence and progress. CILECT is committed to developing and promoting the highest standards of education, research, and training for film, television, and related media through establishing and organizing global and regional forums for the exchange of artistic, pedagogical, methodological, and managerial best practices for all its members.

www.cilect.org/

Film in Education Workshops organizes workshops to produce films that support and promote good education whilst making a change in some way. Their intention is to share children's stories and ensure their message reaches as many people as possible.

www.filmineducationworkshops.com/

Film Therapy Resources

Film and Video Based Therapy is a website intended to create a collaboration between filmmakers, psychologists, anthropologists, psychiatrists, and art therapists in forming a discussion about the use of film and video-based therapy. The content of this site is intended to be an appendix to the anthology *Video and Filmmaking as Psychotherapy: Research and Practice* edited by Joshua L. Cohen, J. Lauren Johnson, and Penny Orr and published by Routledge in 2015.

www.filmandvideobasedtherapy.com/about-us/

Article on the Therapeutic Power of Cinema by Bronwyn Robertson (March 29, 2016). "All Things Connect: The Integration of Mindfulness, Cinema and Psychotherapy." *Counseling Today.*

https://ct.counseling.org/2016/03/all-things-connect-the-integration-of-mindfulness-cinema-and-psychotherapy/

Article on the Healing Functions of Cinema by William Van Omum (March 14, 2012). "Cinematherapy." *American Mental Health Foundation.*

http://americanmentalhealthfoundation.org/2012/03/cinematherapy/

Article on Cinematherapy by Ahmed Hankir, David Holloway, Rashid Zaman, and Mark Agius (2015; Vol. 27, Suppl. 1, pp. 136–142) "Cinematherapy and Film as an Educational Tool in Undergraduate Psychiatry Teaching: A Case Report and Review of the Literature." *Psychiatria Danubina.*

https://pdfs.semanticscholar.org/0404/9fca1288e2d51cf84404adbe69115a9ac9d8.pdf

Article on the Therapeutic Power of Film by Joseph Rauch (April 17, 2017). "14 Movies about Depression that Perfectly Capture the Experience." *Talk Space.*

www.talkspace.com/blog/2017/04/14-movies-about-depression-that-perfectly-capture-the-experience/

Questions for Discussion

- Should you have an online resource section in your project?
- What searches could be performed to find more resources?

INDEX

Printed in Great Britain
by Amazon

82875806R00108